My Life
My Trees

My Life My Trees

Richard St. Barbe Baker

FINDHORN
PRESS

(c) 1970 Richard St Barbe Baker
First published 1970, Lutterworth Press
First paperback edition 1979, The Findhorn Press
Second printing 1981
Second edition 1985
ISBN 0 905249 63 1

Cover design by Claudia Klingemann

Set in 11/12 point Journal Roman
by Findhorn Publications
Printed and bound by Biddles Ltd, UK
Published by The Findhorn Press
The Park, Forres IV36 OTZ, Scotland

TO KATHARINE

ACKNOWLEDGMENTS

It is quite impossible to thank adequately and by name the numerous kind people who have helped me with this book. However two people in particular must be mentioned, for without their co-operation the book would not have been written: Mrs. Gladys Collyer, who magically transcribed my atrocious handwriting and bore with my many additions, alterations and corrections, and Catriona, my wife, who took care of my correspondence and other commitments while I was immersed in my writing.

To my teachers and those who have helped and influenced me in my different spheres of activity I owe a debt of gratitude which can never be repaid.

My thanks are due to the authors and publishers of the quotations I have made and also to the kind friends who have supplied photographs.

CONTENTS

FOREWORD

by Malcolm MacDonald

A BOOK that I have often wished to write is "A Biography of a Tree". It could be a fascinating narrative. I would select some individual young, gracious, characterful tree like an English oak, and as I watched it over the next several decades describe not only its gradual growth and changes of appearance through successive seasons, but also many of the other phenomena whose existences were intermingled with its own: the insects to whom it gave lodging, the rainstorms and sunshine which alternately assaulted it, the human beings who picnicked, gossiped and made love beneath its shade, and every other intimate association with its life . . . But alas! I am myself now too antique to begin the lengthy study necessary for the production of that literary labour.

And now my appetite for such a work is many times satisfied by my reading of Mr. St. Barbe Baker's autobiography. It is, among other achievements, a story of not one tree but of millions, tens of millions and hundreds of millions of trees of countless different kinds growing—but too often also being cut down—in almost every part of the world. In his early childhood the author's interest in trees was born, and from that moment throughout more than threescore years and ten his keen love for them, and even more his wise understanding of the vitally important services they perform for the well-being of mankind and all other living creatures on this Earth, have made him a uniquely knowledgeable and constructive authority on the subject. The story of the life and work of this supreme "Man of the Trees" in Africa, Europe, America, the Antipodes and elsewhere contained in his volume is as fascinating as it is important, and as fabulous as it is true.

It touches on other aspects of his interests in addition to his crusades against the widespread destruction of trees, which over centuries has robbed the Earth of vast areas of natural richness and created such deserts as the Sahara, the Gobi and others. It recounts movingly, for instance, the intellectual philosophy and spiritual faith which have partly inspired his notable activities. His book is written with gay touches of humour as well as deep sensitiveness, and contains much valuable information on its main theme as well as a quietly reasoned yet passionate plea for widespread revivals of tree planting in regions where this could transform barren spaces once more into fruitful homelands for future, more multitudinous generations of men.

My Life—My Trees contains a message which we would do well to heed, if not for our own sakes then in the vital interests of our children and our children's children, before it is too late.

INTRODUCTION

RICHARD ST. BARBE BAKER is one of the world's most senior conservationists. He has spent his whole life encouraging us to care for the trees as if they were our elder brothers, in the knowledge that when we fell them we are sowing the seeds of future deserts.

I first met Richard St. Barbe Baker many years ago at a conference at the Adult Education Centre in Attingham Park, Shrewsbury, where he was being honoured for *Sahara Conquest* which had been acclaimed the book of the month. At that time I thought he was only interested in trees and not spiritual matters. However, I finally wrote to him in New Zealand and sent a copy of Eileen's book, *God Spoke to Me*. To my delight I found that he too put the spiritual life first. Thus when he came to visit Findhorn, he was likewise delighted to find that here was a spiritually based community dedicated to co-operating with nature.

St. Barbe Baker has visited the Findhorn community regularly since its inception, inspiring us in our work and imbuing us with his unique warmth. He has given us much practical advice on the planting of trees and has designed shelter belts to protect us from the strong Scottish winds. At one point he made the suggestion that we move the whole of the community to the Sahara and establish ourselves there in caravans to help reclaim the desert—he was disappointed when I respectfully declined, explaining that our work was to remain based here at Findhorn. We like to think, however, that we are helping to bring to fruition some of the ideals for which he has fought for so many years.

St. Barbe Baker has long been aware of the presence of the Devas and the help that he has received from them. During his visit to Findhorn the Leylands Cypress Deva gave the following message through Dorothy Maclean:

"There is high rejoicing in our kingdoms as the Man of the Trees, so beloved of us, links with you here. Is it not an example in your worlds, that it *is* one world, one work, one cause under God, being expressed through different channels?

I am speaking on behalf of all the tree devas, who have long been overlighting the Man of the Trees, and we wish to express our deepest thanks to him. We hope he has always known of our gratitude for what he has done for us. We should just like to emphasise it in this way. He brings hope for all the world's future. What contribution could be greater?

You understand better now why we have gone on and on about the need for trees on the surface of the earth. Great forests must flourish, and man must see to this if he wishes to continue to live on this planet. The knowledge of this necessity must become part of his consciousness, as much accepted as that he needs water with which to live. He needs trees just as much; the two are linked. We are indeed the skin of the earth, and a skin not only covers and protects but passes through it the forces of life. Nothing could be more vital to life as a whole than trees, trees, and more trees."

In the last decade we have begun to realise just how much we have degraded our planetary home. There has been a phenomenal growth of environmental awareness, and a host of new initiatives have sprung up, whose aim is to bring healing to a sick planet. The Findhorn Community is one such initiative, having the task of demonstrating that mankind does have a future if it can but work hand in hand with nature.

Why cannot we treat planet earth as a sentient being capable of being hurt, just like a human being, when we mistreat it? Mankind has been despoiling the Earth for thousands of years, and now 43% of the world's land surface is covered by desert. The author has called on us to unite as one human race and reclaim these wastelands to heal the Earth so that it can sustain our descendants in the future. If we at Findhorn can turn a barren stretch of sandy coastline into a wonderful garden possessing rich soils, there does not seem to be any reason why all of us can't repair the damage done to the Earth and make it a beautiful place once again.

The focus of Findhorn is global and the Findhorn Community is international in character. From one small caravan and three people, the community has grown to quite a few more caravans and buildings and three hundred people, dedicated not just to talking about the new world they would like to live in, but building it with their own hands. Every year, visitors of all ages and from all walks of life come to a caravan park in the north of Scotland to see a new way of doing things. When we care for the Earth, it cares for us, and when we work together as one human family, no matter what our race, colour or creed, wonderful things can happen. St. Barbe's formula seems to work well for us. And if he had not invented the modern caravan after the First World War, the story of Findhorn might well have been very different.

Last year we were walking together around the Findhorn garden, and I asked him if he remembered his first visit to Findhorn. "1952," his answer came back as sharp as a rifle crack. "But St. Barbe," I said, "Findhorn didn't start until 1962." He turned and looked at me intensely for a moment and then said "Before I led the first Sahara University Ecological Survey in 1952, I came to the Culbin Sands just across the bay to test out my Desert Humber. The year after that I brought my children sailing here."

Richard St. Barbe Baker's links with Findhorn seem to be older than ours, and we are very proud to be able to republish his autobiography. Here is the life of an Earth-healer, struggling against apathy, indifference and plain greed—a man ahead of his time. We love him dearly and recognise him as one of the great souls of our age.

St. Barbe has led a long full life, and one is struck not only by his single-mindedness, but also by his seemingly endless energy. Since this book was first published in 1970, he has been relentlessly carrying on his campaign to reclaim the Sahara, and conserve the world's last existing forests, particularly the Redwoods of California. I am sure he will continue until he drops. The fight is never ending, and we are challenged by this book to stand up and be counted for or against the conservation of our planet. If one man can do so much, what couldn't we achieve if all of us worked together?

PETER CADDY

PREFACE

I AM NOT a professional writer but a planter of trees. An autobiography is perhaps like a coffin—the last thing one needs.

In this book I have tried to record some of the numerous experiments of my life; indeed I am vividly aware that life is one continuous experiment. I would like to feel that what I have been permitted to achieve in conservation and as an Earth Healer through a life-long planting of trees may encourage many others to dedicate their lives to the service of the earth.

I acknowledge with gratitude my teachers and co-workers in the field of silviculture and land reclamation. Any success for which I have been given credit has been the result of teamwork. As I look back on the past the more I realize my personal limitations.

With Rumi the Persian poet I would agree:

When thou madest me to tread
On the path of faith
Thy trust on my back was laid
To be true till death

To me each day is more wonderful than the previous one and my wish for the reader is that he or she may enjoy that same experience.

R. ST. BARBE BAKER

Caius College
Cambridge

Chapter 1

I AM LED FORTH

In sleep of helpless infancy
Trees were the arms that cradled me;
On Tree my daily food is spread,
Tree is my chair and Tree my bed.

TERESA HOOLEY

I WAS BORN in the country in a house on a sunny hill on the fringe of a pine wood in the south of Hampshire. Beacon Hill it was called because just above the house there had been the old tele-graph station with high wooden arms which signalled messages—in twelve minutes—between the Admiralty in London and Portsmouth.

As soon as I could walk I used to sit in a sunny spot on the pine needles and listen to the soft sounds of the wind in their make-shift leaves. It was like music to me. When I was two I had my first little garden. The first things I grew were nasturtiums and soon after that with the help of my Nanny I scratched my name in the soil and sowed white mustard seed. A week later I was proud to spell out the letters of a green RICHARD.

At four with the help of an old sailor I rigged up a little flag pole made from a larch that grew in the wood. I was proud of my flag pole which I had barked and painted myself; it was the centre of the little garden. Each morning I hoisted a flag and each evening I took it down, carefully rolled it up and tied it correctly ready to hoist and 'break' the next day. At the entrance to my little garden I stuck two withies and made an arch just big enough to allow me to pass under it. In a month's time to my great delight they started to grow leaves. It was a great thrill, for until then I had not grown anything more ambitious than nasturtiums and mustard.

When I was given a wheelbarrow I used to collect leaves from an oak wood at the end of the garden. I dug a little pit up to my waist and gradually filled it with layers of leaves, covering this with road scrapings and stable manure from our pony, and finally topped it with inverted slabs of turf.

I watched my father bud roses in the summer and graft pears and apples in the winter. He allowed me to tie the buds in with wet raffia grass from an iron bowl. I became quite expert at this and soon I was allowed to prepare the bud myself. If the graft on an apple stock had not taken there was a chance to bud it later. I loved doing this and vied with the gardeners in getting the best results.

On Saturday evenings instead of playing cricket, as a great treat I was allowed to help my father sow tree seeds in long narrow beds I had helped to make. As the little pine seedlings came up they wore a little 'cap' which they seemed to be raising in salute.

I was fascinated by the regiments of tiny seedlings and I protected, weeded and watered them. Their care was more important to me than any game.

At the age of four I used my father's tools and my first effort in carpentering was to make a soap box for my mother, used for many years in the scullery sink and afterwards for further years at the stables.

My forebears had originally lived in Kent, having been granted lands by Henry I who married off one of his paramours to a young knight. For generations Sissinghurst Castle was the Baker home until it was commandeered and used as an internment camp for French prisoners of war, who eventually burnt it down. It was then that the family were scattered and my branch went to live at Cawston in Norfolk. The Bakers who came from Normandy frequently intermarried with the St. Barbes who came from Brittany. Generations of St. Barbes lived at Broadlands, Romsey, until it was sold to Lord Palmerson, in Victorian times.

I was interested to find in the Pembroke College Library a family entry on p. 128, *Venn Aluni Cantabrigeenses* Volume I, Pt. 2:

Richard Baker admitted at Pembroke, March 7th, 1758, son of Richard Baker, Esq., of Yarmouth, Norfolk, born there, Matriculated, Michaelmas 1758; Scholar; B.A. 1762; M.A. 1765; D.D. 1788. Fellow 1763. Ordained Priest, London, February 19th, 1769. Rector of Great Poringland, Norfolk, 1772-9; Rector of Cawstone 1772-1818. A friend and contemporary of the poet, Gray, and one of the three fellows of the College who witnessed the signing of Gray's Will, July 2nd, 1770. Author of The Harmony or

Argument of the Four Evangelists (in four parts). The Psalms of David
Evangelised. Died April 16th, 1818, aged 77. Father of Richard 1790.
Vol. II. 309. Gave the picture by Berochio in the Chapel. This beautiful
sacred painting is of Joseph of Arimathea claiming the body of Christ
being taken down from the Cross—it forms the reredos behind the com-
munion table in the College Chapel. His son Richard Baker was admitted
to Pembroke at the age of 16, June 30th, 1790, as Baker (sic) Richard son
and heir of Richard 1758 Clerk, D.D., Rector of Cawstone, Norfolk, born
there. Matriculated Michaelmas 1791; Scholar; B.A. 1795. M.A. 1800.
Ordained deacon (Norwich), February 2, 1796; Priest, December 22nd,
1799. Rector of Botley, Hants, 1803-54, Died December 5th, 1854, aged
81 years, at Botley, Father of the next, James Scott (1822), and John
Thomas Wright (1830) and Stephen C. (1833).

As a boy I was told of my great-grandfather, Rector of Botley,
Hampshire, for fifty-two years, who was one of the old-fashioned
type of sporting parson. He used to wear a pink coat under a black
gown, and he encouraged sport of every kind. He thought nothing
of riding the seventy miles to London for a luncheon engagement,
returning the next day. In order to promote the noble art of self-
defence, a barrel of home-brewed beer was rolled out of the rectory
on a Sunday afternoon in support of the local champion who would
challenge all comers from Portsmouth.

He was a good boxer himself, as two highwaymen discovered
one evening when they tried to relieve him of the money he was
carrying home for his servants' wages. It was two footpads to one
old man and a dog, and the Rector was attacked from front and
back. But he got the better of his assailants, and with the help of
his dog he marched them to the Bargate at Southampton. Then he
walked home to Botley, arriving at the rectory cool and unper-
turbed, though his white shirt-front was covered in blood!

A former Scholar and Fellow of Pembroke College, Cambridge,
he had earlier exchanged his living at Cawston in Norfolk for the
one at Botley. He drove the whole two hundred miles in the family
coach, borrowing horses at various stages, until he reached his new
rectory. Then the coach was left in a paddock, where it became
family mansion for generations of free-ranging cocks and hens.

Great-grandfather Baker is buried in the family vault at the west
end of Botley church. It is an ornate affair with a pointed pillar

bearing the family coat of arms. The present Rector, the Reverend Duke Baker, told me that once when the Sunday School was leaving the church, one little fellow pointed to the vault and asked, "Is that where Jesus was buried?"

His eldest son, my great-uncle Richard, was a scholar too and coached his brothers for Cambridge. For a while he farmed the 800-acre glebe farm for his father, riding once a year to Norfolk to collect rent from tenants on the family estate. Then he decided upon a more adventurous life, so he went out to Ontario, Canada, where he cleared the bush and shot wild bear.

His nearest neighbour, George, lived seven miles away, and on Sunday afternoons it was Richard's custom to ride over to visit his friends. As a boy of ten, I used to find it thrilling to listen to letters read to me by my father, which he too had enjoyed as a ten-year-old. Long passages of these letters dealt with philosophical and religious questions, often in an introspective vein, but every now and then there would be a spicy bit about bears. It was then that I sat up and really took notice.

One incident stands out in my memory. George told Richard how one night he heard an alarming noise coming from the yard. Pulling a sheepskin coat over his nightshirt, he went out into the yard, and there was a big black bear struggling to lift his prize hog over the sty . . . He had no rifle or gun with him, so he seized a spade and with one mighty blow laid the bear's skull open with the edge, killing it. It fell dead at his feet.

Dead at his feet! I kissed my mother and said good night to her and my father. Looking out from my bedroom window I could see my young trees in the moonlight. I searched in all directions, but there was not even a shadow that remotely resembled a bear. "I will go to Canada one day," I thought, "where I can kill bears with spades!"

Richard's brother was John Thomas Wright Baker, my grandfather. He went to Clare Hall (now Clare College) and, like his father, became a parson. He did duty at the Hampshire parishes of Botley, Durley, Sholing, and West End, where he lived in his own house with a large, tree-surrounded garden. Like Nelson's Admiral Collingwood, he would tuck acorns in the hedgerows along the fields of his parish. Seventy years afterwards many of the resulting fine oaks were felled to build the little rescue ships of the war.

He was a great walker—it is recorded that he once walked forty-two miles before breakfast on a pint of beer—and always undertook his pastoral visits on foot, except on Sundays when he was driven in a brougham. He was also a trained athlete and excelled at both high and long jump. Sometimes when my father and grandmother were driving in the chaise they would meet my grandfather returning from some visit. For fun, he would start running backwards in front of the fast-trotting pony and at every dozen strides or so would jump backwards over his walking-stick!

He had a reputation as an eloquent reader, and rich and poor would fill his churches to hear him bring to life the ancient characters of Scripture for their enlightenment and enchantment.

It seems that in his church views he was led towards evangelicalism by his forebear, that author of *The Penitential Psalsm of David*. He could not abide sacerdotalism and avoided using the word "altar" for the "Lord's Table", adhering strictly to the Church's rubrics. A life-long vegetarian, he considered the Lord's Supper a love-feast of bread and wine among His close followers, as he believed the Master had meant it to be.

His out-and-out evangelical attitude was frowned upon by his Bishop who wrote him a curt note on the subject. Being of a highly sensitive nature he was so deeply shocked by this unchristian reproof that the blood rushed to his head, and he dropped dead. He was buried in the graveyard near the west door of the church at West End, where later my grandmother was buried too.

My dear father, John Richard St. Barbe Baker, the only child, was fourteen at the time, and from then on his gentle mother, who had felt the blow most bitterly, became his responsibility. He devoted himself to her and to his woodlands, establishing forest nurseries, and training and employing a number of men.

He had been brought up to understand that the family money, which his aunt Sarah had the use of during her lifetime, would ensure his independence. At the time of her last illness he was spending his winter doing missionary work among the villagers of the mountains of Southern France. In response to a telegram, he returned just in time to be with the old lady and comfort her in death. When the will came to be read, however, it was found that the family trustees had persuaded Aunt Sarah to leave most of the money to them. My father asked his lawyer cousin's advice, and they both took the view that it was God's will and therefore little use throwing the matter into chancery.

The trustees, who were brothers and also bankers, retired on Aunt Sarah's money. The senior one bought a mansion in the country, furnished and equipped with servants. On the very first morning after his arrival to take possession, the butler came in to draw the curtains. When there was no reply to his comment on the weather, he went over to the bed, where he found his new master— dead. He telegraphed the brother, who at once caught a train from London. He asked the guard to stop at a halt near his brother's mansion, so that he could take a short cut across the fields. As requested, the train stopped. Nobody alighted, so the guard walked along the train—to find the younger brother dead in his seat.

My father agreed with his cousin that this looked like divine retribution, but the misdirected wealth still did not return to him, so he gave up all thought of living as a country gentleman and turned his hobby into his business. This was fortunate for me, for from earliest childhood I became intimate with trees in nurseries.

As a boy, my father had not followed the family tradition of going to Cambridge; he had instead a private tutor. At the age of seventeen he became interested in the Evangelical Revival of the eighties of the last century, and under the influence of Archbishop Chenevix Trench's daughter devoted himself to God's work, volunteering to carry on when Miss Trench left the district. Though he was only eighteen he filled the village reading-room on Sunday afternoons and evenings. Later, he built a Mission Hall seating three hundred in his own garden. People from the surrounding villages came to this centre—soon even missionaries from Africa and India.

It was about this time that my father proposed to the only daughter of the Squire. Charlotte Purrott had played the harmonium in her father's reading-room and enthusiastically helped Miss Trench and John Baker with the Mission services. It was she who had been Miss Agnes Weston's strong supporter when she founded her Mission to Seamen. Charlotte's father, who was the Vicar's

Warden at West End, kept the best horses in that part of Hampshire and hunted with the Hursley and the New Forest Stag Hounds. Although his daughter never hunted, he mounted her well.

When my father asked her to marry him she said that, fond as she was of him, she could not possibly marry him as he would not be able to provide her with the kind of life she had been accustomed to enjoy.

A few weeks later her father lost his money in the Devil's Dyke Railway Company. Charles Purrott had believed in the Australian claimant in the Tichborne case and, having promised his support, lost heavily when the case was not proved. He was perhaps forty years ahead of his time in this venture. The combination of these unfortunate investments cost him his house and property at West End. Servants went, horses went, and his beautiful house too. His daughter wrote to my father:

"Dear John,
My father has lost all his money. Please marry me."
And he did.

I was fortunate in having a charming grandmother who used to take me for walks to visit her old neighbours. Those were the days of polite calls and daintily served tea in china cups. One Tuesday afternoon when we were calling upon her nearest neighbour, Mrs. Anderson, we found her distressed because she had lost a little tabby kitten. My grandmother mentioned that on Sunday evening a little stray kitten had come to the house. It had probably followed one of the maids to the Mission Hall. I had befriended it and it had settled down and become one of the family. I was terribly afraid that I might have to give up my kitten to which I had become very attached. Happily Mrs. Anderson sensed my anxiety and asked me, "Do you love my little kitten very much?" I answered that I did and so she generously said I might keep it. That was the first and last call that afternoon. I hastened home to make sure that my kitten was safe.

I was now four. My father was adding a couple of rooms to his house and I spent much time with the carpenters. Having seen a funeral procession the week before, when my father had put on his frock coat and a black silk hat, I was taken with the notion that if my pussy were to die I must give her a proper funeral with a coffin. I made a box two feet long from ends of flooring—even at that early age I could use tools with precision and drive nails. I fitted a lid with leather hinges and tarred it inside and out, plastering myself at the same time. I remember my nanny making me rub butter on my hands to remove the black sticky stuff before finally scrubbing my hands with soap and water. The kitten's coffin was put into the roof of the shed where it stayed until the cowman broke a leg off the milk stool. Then my black box served him instead for many years. My kitten lived to be thirteen and in the end walked off into the wood. I always thought she had a secret burial place, but search as I might I never found it.

When I was five my father said, "You are getting a big boy now. This will make you strong," and he cut a slice of meat from the servants' joint. Although he was practically vegetarian himself, he provided a weekly joint for the cook and the housemaids.

"Father, I don't need it," I protested, and soon ate up the vegetables and baked potato.

"But Daddy says you must eat it—take it to your room and do not come down till it's gone!"

It was a beautiful Saturday and it seemed unfair that I should be punished in this way. Every now and again my father would call up the stairs, "My boy! Has that meat gone?"

"No, father," I would have to admit.

I looked out across the lawn to my seed beds where whole regiments of little trees were awaiting my attention, and as my eyes ranged nearer I saw my kitten on the lawn just under my window. In a loud whisper I called, "Kitty," and threw out that horrid slice of beef. She snapped it up. A great fear came over me. I crouched on the floor beside my bed in the corner waiting in terror of what might happen next. After a seemingly interminable time, the voice came again:

"My boy! Has that meat gone?"

"Y-y-y-e-s, Father," I called back tremblingly.

"Good boy. You may come down."

I escaped to my little trees and a hot tear dropped into the watering can, for I had deceived my father whom I loved. I never had the courage to own up to what I had done. He had been obeyed, at least so he thought, and that was what mattered to him. He never tried to make me eat meat again and I proved for myself that it was not necessary as a food. My health was good. I was strong, and as I grew up I could walk or ride long distances.

My father could not abide sectarianism and each month held a united prayer-meeting to which he welcomed ministers of all denominations. In the atmosphere of prayer their religious differences vanished, for with their convenor they all acknowledged the Fatherhood of God and the Brotherhood of Man. To his hospitable home came Hindus and Buddhists, Persian Sufis, devout followers of Islam and missionaries on furlough.

In the high summer of 1894 I had an unforgettable experience which at the early age of five altered my outlook on life and I believe more than anything influenced the way by which I have come.

As I have already explained, my earliest and happiest memories are bound up with trees. One of the earliest is that of the pine forest which came up close to the house. I often sat in the sun there and in the tree tops I seemed to hear the sound of waves breaking on the sea-shore. Those pines spoke to me of distant lands and gave me my first desire to travel and see the trees of other countries. At times I would imagine that these tall pines were talking to each other as they shook or nodded their heads at the whim of the winds. I did not know then that I would be at school with James Elroy Flecker who once wrote:

"For pines are gossip pines the wide world through."

My old nurse, Perrin, was a real native of Hampshire. As a girl she used to glean in the fields and get sufficient wheat she told me, to keep them in bread for the year. She was married to a forester in charge of woodlands belonging to Queen's College, Oxford. These woodlands adjoined my father's estate, and from my earliest days my nurse took me for walks there. I loved the Perrin cottage; it was on a knoll on the fringe of the woods and from it I could peer into the dark woods of "dreamy gloomy friendly trees". That pine forest was full of romance and boyish adventure for me.

A stone's throw from the cottage was a large brick oven, where the weekly batch of bread was baked. I often watched spellbound to see the hot, sweet-smelling loaves removed from the oven. To me Perrin was a sort of High Priestess officiating at her altar and the scent of the burning gorse seemed like incense to me. When I was small it was the huge sandpit that provided the greatest attraction for me. It was in full sight of the oven and I usually played in it on baking days. It was there that I made my first attempt at treescaping. I collected twigs of pines broken off by squirrels or the wind and stuck them into mounds of sand. I planted an avenue leading up to a sand-castle, complete with drawbridge and moat. My early treescaping efforts were influenced to some extent by the attractive coloured slides shown by my father.

The surrounding woods were extensive and in those days I never penetrated very far, nor would Perrin take me into the forest as a rule. To a small boy their depths were mysterious and rather awe-inspiring. One day, I found I had exhausted my ideas of treescaping in the sandpit and so, greatly daring, asked if I might be allowed to go for a walk in the wood. Perrin said the woods were full of adders at this time of the year and no safe place for the likes of a small boy. But I coaxed her to let me go and reluctantly she allowed me to set out on what seemed to me a wonderful expedition. No explorer of space probing the secrets of other planets could have felt more exultation than I did at that moment.

As I set out on that greatest of all forest adventures, at first I kept to a path which wound its way down into the valley; but soon I found myself in a dense part of the forest where the trees were taller and the path became lost in bracken beneath the pines. Soon I was completely isolated in the luxuriant, tangled growth of ferns which were well above my head. In my infant mind I seemed to have entered the fairyland of my dreams. I wandered on as in a dream, all sense of time and space lost. As I continued this mysterious journey, looking up every now and then I could see shafts of light where the sunshine lit up the morning mists and made subtle shadows on the huge bracken fronds which provided a continuous canopy of bright green over me. Their pungent scent was a delight to me. Although I could see only a few yards ahead, I had no sense of being shut in. The sensation was exhilerating. I began to walk faster, buoyed up with an almost ethereal feeling of well-being, as if I had been detached from earth. I became intoxicated with the beauty around me, immersed in the joyousness and exultation of feeling part of it all.

Soon the bracken became shorter, and before long it was left behind as a clearing opened where the dry pine needles covered the floor of the forest with a soft brown carpet. Rays of light pierced the canopy of the forest, were reflected in the ground mists and appeared as glorious shafts interlaced with the tall stems of the trees; bright and dark threads woven into a design. I had entered the temple of the woods. I sank to the ground in a state of ecstasy; everything was intensely vivid—the call of a distant cuckoo seemed just by me. I was alone and yet encompassed by all the living creatures I loved so dearly.

As I lay back a dead twig snapped, like the crack of a whip; the birds warbling sounded like the notes of a cathedral organ. The overpowering beauty of it all entered my very being. At that moment my heart brimmed over with a sense of unspeakable thankfulness which has followed me through the years since that woodland re-birth. My gratitude for this cosmic experience can be perhaps best expressed in the Scots' metrical version of the Twenty-third Psalm:

> *Goodness and Mercy all my life,*
> *Shall surely follow me:*
> *And in God's house for evermore,*
> *My dwelling-place shall be.*

I was lost in the depths of the forest, but at that moment this did not dawn upon me. I was conscious of a feeling of bliss only once repeated in my childhood.

The second experience was when my father, in a lantern lecture on Bunyan's *Pilgrim's Progress*, threw on the screen a picture of Beulah Land. With a hundred and fifty others I sang the hymn:

> *O! Beulah land,*
> *Sweet Beulah land,*
> *As on the highest mount I stand*

And gaze away across the sea
Where mansions are prepared for me,
I view the shining glory shore
My heaven, my home for evermore.

In the wood among the pines, it seemed that for one brief moment I had tasted immortality, and in a few seconds had lived an eternity. This experience may last for ever.

Just beyond the tall pines was another trail where I turned to the left. In a few minutes I was back with Perrin and the common-place things of daily life—the washing and the baking. But how everything in this short interval had changed; even the clothes hanging out to dry on the line tied between two pines seemed like gay flags hung out for a coronation. I watched red-faced old Perrin taking out the most wonderful loaves from the brick oven. Close to her side, I walked home to the midday meal as if treading on air. I no longer minded the big black dog that used to bark so furiously at us. Even Rasey, the cross old gardener, looked like a favourite uncle to me. I seemed to sense the affection of my parents as never before. I was in love with life; I was indeed born again, although I could not have explained what had happened to me then.

The next day I went back to the woods. They now held a new and strange fascination for me. Perrin gave her consent more readily but added her usual caution, "Keep out of harm's way." I used to wonder why it was that Perrin never seemed to want to go into the woods and never, never encouraged me to venture very far. With her it was always those adders, or the 'obidyois and the little folk'.

It was a bright sunny day and this time I kept to the woodland path which brought me out to some younger plantations. I tried to find the place where I had been the day before, but, though I must have been very close, it evaded me, nor did I again experience the rapture of the previous day.

After a while I used to explore different parts of the woods. I left the pines and ventured into a beech wood. On the fringe of the beeches I could get a clear view of Winchester, twelve miles away. On good days I could see St. Catherine's Hill, where we

sometimes went for picnics near a clump of beeches. There was a
huge maze cut in the ground and I and my brother Scott used to
race each other to the middle, which took about eight minutes,
and out again. We were told that it had been cut by a boy at
Winchester School who had been kept back at the end of term as a
punishment. It was said that he had cut this huge maze with his
penknife, then died of a broken heart singing *Dulce domum*. That
story used to make me feel sad and unhappy; I entered into his
distress at being prevented from returning home for the holidays.
But when I was feeling unhappy, or if things had gone wrong for
me during the day, I would leave the house, run down the little
lane, cross the meadow and visit a particular beech tree in the
wood. That beech with smooth bark was a Mother Confessor to
me—my Madonna of the Woods. Standing by the friendly beech, I
knew in my heart that my troubles and my grief, as well as all that
pleased me, were but for a passing moment. I would imagine that
I had roots digging down deep into Mother Earth and that all
above I was sprouting branches. I would hold that in my thoughts
for a few moments and then come back with the strength of the
tree and a radiant heart, knowing that that was all that really
mattered. John Masefield's inspired *Terra Incognita* in *Lollington
Downs and Other Poems, 1917*, expresses my feeling:

> *Here in the self is all that man can know*
> *Of Beauty, all the wonder, all the power,*
> *All the unearthly colour, all the glow,*
> *Here in the self which withers like a flower;*
> *Here in the self which fades as hours pass,*
> *And droops and dies and rots and is forgotten*
> *Sooner, by ages, than the mirroring glass*
> *In which it sees its glory still unrotten . . .*
> *Beauty herself, the universal mind,*
> *Eternal April wandering alone;*
> *The God, the Holy Ghost, the atoning Lord,*
> *Here in the flesh, the never yet explored.*

From that moment life became exciting and I entered with zest
into the Sunday services and helped my father at the week-night

meetings. The Mission Hall on Beacon Hill opened its doors to the workless in the dark days of unemployment and became a shining spiritual beacon. Coffee suppers were served and illustrated talks on Bunyan's *Pilgrim's Progress* listened to with rapt attention. By the age of twelve I was sometimes called upon to deputize for my father. In time, I and my brother, Scott, used to walk the five miles to Curdridge Church for the morning service and some Sundays to Bitterne, two miles in another direction, for the evening service. On my return after supper, my father would ask me to read *Spurgeon's Sermons* to him. Having given out all day he liked to hear a sermon from *The Christian Herald* or perhaps an article on prophecy from *The English Churchman*.

Regularly once a month the Reverend Melville Churchill, cousin of Sir Winston, and erudite contributor to *The English Churchman* under the name of 'M.A. Cantab', used to walk the eight miles from his home in Bishops Waltham to visit us. He was in sympathy with my father's evangelical work and he too had built a Mission Hall. He had a weakness for the perfectly made *moka* coffee my father had learned to make during the winters he had spent as a child in France. The books of Daniel and Revelation provided these earnest students of prophecy with dates which seemed to confirm past happenings and led them to look for future fulfilment. I was fascinated by their exciting conclusions when substituting a year for a day.

Towards the end of the Boer War when Mr. Churchill arrived for his monthly discussion, my father greeted him with, "That young cousin of yours in South Africa is a bit of a harum scarum, isn't he?"

"You might think so, John, but Winston keeps his parents with his war stories in *The Daily Telegraph*. Mark my word, John, one day he will be Prime Minister of England."

Many were the famous preachers who visited my father to preach in the Mission Hall. I always remember General Booth, the Founder of the Salvation Army, discussing the progress of the soul with my father one Sunday evening after supper. The General maintained that backsliding would be forgiven twice but never a third time. To illustrate his point he knelt by a chair and, holding up his thumb and first two fingers said, "Mr. Baker, here's the soul," while I watched with intense interest, taking for granted the soul was there. He placed his thumb and fingers on the chair and brought them across to somewhere near the middle and suddenly drew them back.

"There, Mr. Baker," he said, "that's once." Again he advanced the imaginary soul to somewhere near the edge of the chair, then withdrew it, looking fiercely at my father.

"That, Mr. Baker, is the second time." The third time he passed his fingers and thumb to the edge of the chair and brought them down to the floor with a thump. I was so hypnotized by the General and in sympathy with the poor soul I too fell flat on my face on the floor. The General continued to lay down the law, while my father pleaded with him that God was able to forgive until seventy times seven. But the General would have none of this—he had his own rules for salvation.

It was in this atmosphere that I was brought up to wait on the guests and run errands for my father. As the eldest of a family of five I became responsible at an early age.

My first school was in the neighbouring village of Bitterne which I walked to, making a short cut through an adjoining property, until I was seven, when I had my first bicycle—a heavy frame affair with cushion tyres. During the holidays I went for long rides throughout the New Forest and our part of the county.

One of our neighbours kept bees and one day I watched him manipulate a hive. When he took out a bar-frame covered with bees I asked him to let me hold it. I was thrilled with the sight and when I went home I asked my father if he would give me a hive. After some days, when he found that my heart was set on keeping bees, he suggested that I might exchange some of my apple trees that I had myself grafted for a stock.

This was when I was twelve. By the time I was sixteen I had become a proficient bee-master, with sixteen hives, the best of which in a single season yielded me two hundred and forty pounds of honey. I built up my apiary with driven bees which I rescued from the cottagers' sulphur pits. My modern bar-framed hives I had made in my own workshop after the model of the first one I had bought.

I am always grateful to my parents for allowing me to have my own garden at an early age and build a little house of my own and later a revolving summer house for my mother. It seemed natural for me to do these things and I would have felt frustrated if prevented. My father believed that whatever a man's profession he should still be able to keep himself and his family by manual labour. I have proved for myself the soundness of this theory, having worked my way through three Universities, and been given an honorary degree at the first forestry school in the U.S.A. for my contribution in creating employment on the land for six million young men. I have always found it a distinct advantage to be able to show someone how to do a job, instead of issuing orders on paper.

There is another aspect of life on the land; while working in forest or garden a man has time for meditation and indeed his very act is devotion. He becomes in tune with the Infinite. The miracle of growth and the seasons' changes induce a sense of wonderment and call forth worship from his inner being and in this sense WORK becomes WORSHIP.

Although my father had had a tutor he decided that if at all possible I should go to a Public School and he was concerned that it should be one with Evangelical tendencies. No doubt he discussed this with the Rev. Melville Churchill; so in 1902, when I was thirteen, I was sent to Dean Close School, Cheltenham. The Headmaster was a German Jew by the name of Flecker, who had married a Russian Jewess. Both were clever. Their eldest son, James Elroy, became a poet and wrote *Hassan*.

My dear mother came to my first Speech Day and seemed to be spending a lot of time with Mrs. Flecker. On the first night of the holidays after she had heard me say my prayers, she said:

"My dear boy, I do hope you have nothing to do with Elroy Flecker—his mother was unburdening her heart to me about the trouble he has been to her and his dear father." Elroy had already gone up to Oxford but he brought cricket teams to play the school. After my mother's warning I thought I would investigate for myself and become friendly with him, although he was rather a recluse.

While I was at school at Cheltenham I was fortunate enough to get to know the Elwes family at Colesbourne, about six miles away in the Cotswolds. It was a wooded estate of about seven thousand acres and there I would often spend my half-term or good conduct holidays. The owner of these extensive woodlands was writing a book on *Trees of Great Britain and Ireland*, assisted by Professor Henry, the Cambridge botanist, who had spent much time collecting rare species in China. Henry too would sometimes stay at Colesbourne and I would be allowed to accompany them on their forestry and botanical expeditions.

On one of these Henry pointed out to Elwes rather a special variety of elm. He was not at all dogmatic but only tentatively put this suggestion forward. "I don't agree with you," said Elwes, whereupon Henry attempted to point out the very slight botanical variation and handed his pocket magnifying lens to Elwes so that he could better examine the flower of the tree for himself.

"I don't agree with you, Henry," repeated Elwes. "Now if you would only listen to me," and he gave his own opinion at some length. Naturally Henry listened but said no more. The following day I was walking alone with Elwes. As we came to the elm tree discussed on the previous day, Elwes took up a stance, undid his coat, hooked his thumbs in his waistcoat, faced the elm and addressed me in rather a fierce tone of voice:

"Baker, this elm is not what you think it is. I have made a discovery: far from being a common English elm, *Ulmus campestris*, this is likely to be related to the Huntingdon elm, and if you are not convinced that I am right I would ask you to examine the flower, when you will discover for yourself that my opinion is correct."

Had Elwes forgotten that I had listened to the argument the day before or was it his way of instructing me on the identification of forest trees? Years afterwards on my return from Africa, it was my good fortune to stay at Colesbourne with his son Colonel Elwes and become more intimate with the woodlands and the family. Many were the days I devoted to forestry there.

While I was still at Dean Close, a man came to talk about Canada. It was not what he said but what he did that impressed itself on my mind. He wore a tail coat with stiff shirt and collar and ready-made white tie, and at one stage in his lecture he caught hold of his collar and shook it savagely and said, "Out in Canada we don't have to wear these durned things; we wear soft collars or no collars at all!"

My mind was now made up. I *must* go to Canada. After four years I discovered that my father was selling land to pay school fees for my education. He listened gravely when I told him that I knew of his sacrifices and that I wanted to leave school to go to Canada.

Then an old-time pioneer, Bishop Lloyd, returned from the Western Prairies. I was introduced to him by an old friend of my father, Dr. Eugene Stock, Secretary of the Church Missionary Society. Lloyd said he wanted men who would go out ahead of the railway and 'blaze the trail'. He spoke of the scattered settlers far from the towns who had no means of grace, and appealed to me to throw in my lot with a group of undergraduates at Emmanuel College, Saskatchewan University, Saskatoon.

I responded to the call and for the next few months worked hard to equip myself for my mission to Canada. I rose at five and got myself some breakfast before leaving for Southampton, where I was learning how to make horse shoes from short lengths of wrought iron.

One of my father's customers was a young fruit-grower from Burridge where my great-grandfather had owned much land which he had planted with trees. Young Roberts, the fruit-grower had bought some of this land where the timber had been felled and was having it grubbed ready for orchards and fruit gardens. I begged this young man to allow me to go and camp with him and help him lay out his property—I wanted to sleep under the stars and get fit for the work in Canada that lay ahead of me. After the day's work was done we would put on boxing gloves. In those days I rather fancied that I could punch hard—young Roberts was a fine specimen of muscular Christianity and although I had a longer reach he made me hop around. I was always grateful to him for putting me through my paces in preparation for the North-West and have treasured his friendship through the years. After sixty years we still correspond. I had a letter from him at Frith Farm, Wickham, Hampshire, dated January 10, 1969:

Not only did you cook for me, but you did the washing and you carted the fruit by horse and van, besides rushing about in the middle of the night and scaring that Mr. Miles who came down and slept in the tent with us, making out we were being attacked by robbers. And do you remember grinding the corn and making bread in that coal stove in the shed? Not only that, do you remember taking your little harmonium out in the Burridge Road and conducting a service each Sunday? You have always been a wonderful chap, full of good deeds and personality, and one could never keep you down.

You come from a line of saints. I shall never forget your dear mother singing and playing on a little organ—"There is no love like the love of Jesus"—she played so beautifully and she meant every word of it. Both your parents were saints when the time came for them to go, and I think if you had pursued this Evangelistic work, you would have done very great work. I know what great satisfaction you have obtained from your parents.

But to return to the story. For three and a half years I was in the hard school of the open spaces. I homesteaded south of Saskatoon and pitched my tent on Beaver Creek, where in the small hours of the morning I took delight in watching the beavers. They constructed a dam along which I could walk. It was more than one hundred and forty feet in width across a stream which had been less than a dozen feet wide when they had started building. In the winter I returned and was thrilled to find a large beaver house, the top of which protruded three to four feet above the ice. It looked like the crater of a miniature volcano with hot air and steam rising from the summit, upon the fringes of which the snow had melted to become icicles. The beavers' dam had flooded about twelve acres of meadow. From then one, the beavers became my lasting friends and I came to regard them as fellow foresters.

As one of the first hundred students at Saskatchewan University (there are 12,000 students at the University at the time of writing!) I was elected to a committee for drawing up a college yell. After much thought we decided we must combine our colours with the name of the University. This was the result:

Saskatchewan, Saskatchewan, Varsitee!
Hi hickety ki yi! Hi hickety kee!

Deo et patri! Deo et patri!
The green the white! Ki yam i yam i kee!
Sas-s-s-s-s-s-skatchewan!

As sophomores we had the privilege of initiating the freshmen,
and in my sophomore year one of the freshmen was Diefenbaker,
afterwards Prime Minister of Canada.

My knowledge of horses was my best introduction to the
Redskins, among whom social status was governed by the quality
of their horsemanship. They were proud of their horses and always
insisted that I rode their best. There was a happy rivalry between
these friendly Indians who each claimed that they had the best
horse.

Those were my bronco-busting days. In England they talk of
'breaking' a horse while in France they use the verb 'dresser' or
to finish a horse. It is a pity that the old English term to 'gentle'
a horse is so rarely used, and I prefer the word 'make' to 'break'.
In the *Haute Ecole* much attention is given to finding the centre of
gravity of a horse or adjusting one's own weight so that the horse
can enjoy perfect balance. This is the opposite of rodeo when
horses are tortured with a strap or rope drawn tight under the
belly so that they play up and buck to get rid of it or the rider.

Like many another 'tenderfoot' I had a go at riding untamed
broncos. and once when in Pleasant Valley, Alberta, had a beautiful black Montana bronco promised to me if I could ride him. He
was one of a bunch of about eighty wild mustangs and had twice
jumped the corral close on seven feet high. The boss had turned
to me with a curse and exclaimed:

"Say boy, if you can ride that damned black devil, it's yours."

That afternoon I rode him twenty-five miles and returned the
next day to claim him and thank his owner for a wonderful gift.
He was the best journey horse I have ridden and was game for
seventy miles a day. His most comfortable gait was a fast canter
relieved every now and again by a dot-and-carry-one tittup.

I traded beautiful green Hudson Bay blankets with the Indians
for horses and arrived in college with six of them plus a load of

hay. I built a barn on the university campus and a shack near by. My ponies were my best friends and they helped me pay my way through college. I shared my shack with two other university students and contributed a page each week to *The Saturday Press* to buy a meal ticket at a Chinese restaurant.

In the autumn of 1910, while crossing the prairies of Canada, I recognized for the first time a desert in the making. Wide areas had been ploughed up where for centuries dwarf willows had stabilized the deep, rich, black soil. The country had been divided into townships with sections of 640 acres. In those days anybody could file on to a quarter section of 160 acres for nothing, and if he needed more, that could be acquired.

The first thing they did was to plough as much of it as they could, then sow wheat, and oats to feed the horses. One could travel miles without seeing a tree. When a farmer took up a section of land, he would mark the boundary, put up a couple of poles with strips of an old white shirt tied on the tops, so that they could be seen a mile way; sit on the plough with his six-horse outfit and drive straight, keeping the markers between the heads of the leading horses—backwards and forwards on dead level ground, breaking five acres a day. Two crops of wheat would be grown and then a crop of oats. His neighbour would be doing the same. With no sheltering trees the soil began to drift and blow away; up to an inch of soil would be lost in a year.

Years afterwards my secretary, Finlayson, told me of a Dorset farmer who decided to go to Saskatchewan. He took up land, dug a cellar and built a frame house on top of it; ploughed up the prairie and grew wheat and oats. After twenty years he decided the country was no good for farming, for eight feet of his soil had gone and he had to climb up into his house. He could not sell so left it derelict and returned to Dorset, where he became a tenant farmer once again with tree-surrounded fields.

During my three and a half years in the North-West of Canada I encouraged the planting of trees, not only around the homesteads but as shelter belts around the farms and fields. On the Saskatchewan University farm at Sutherland and at Medicine Hat, we had nurseries and experimented with various species to get the best shelter. The Government gave trees freely to farmers.

It was while working in a lumber camp near Prince Albert, swinging the axe as a lumber jack, that my heart was torn to see the unnecessary waste of trees, and I decided that one day I would myself qualify for forestry work.

Having earned enough to return to England I was studying Divinity at Ridley Hall, Cambridge, at the outbreak of World War I. While at Emmanuel College, Saskatchewan, taking arts and sciences, I had devoted myself to Christian work in the North-West and in the building up of congregations of isolated settlers around the central schools of Mission Churches. I felt that before accepting ordination I should gain wider experience and perhaps complete my studies at Cambridge where generations of my forebears had taken their degrees or had become Fellows of their colleges.

Into the peace and seclusion of Ridley Hall came the threat of war. I had taken to heart the Sermon on the Mount and sought the guidance of my tutor, for whom I had the greatest possible admiration. If the teachings of Jesus meant anything and if we were to take up His Cross and follow Him, it would mean throwing up my cavalry training in King Edward's Horse—the King's Overseas Dominions' Regiment—and becoming a conscientious objector to war with all the deprivation it would entail. My tutor, however, explained that the Sermon on the Mount was a counsel of perfection and obviously we could hardly expect to be able to live up to it yet. Besides, Jesus Himself fought the money-changers in the Temple and would wish His followers to steel themselves for the fight against evil. He said: "I came not to bring peace but a sword." Somewhat bewildered this young divinity student decided to go to the summer camp with his regiment. Two weeks later war came, and in response to an appeal I volunteered for immediate service overseas. That was towards the end of the summer in August, 1914.

I had joined up as a trooper in King Edward's Horse, but it was with the guns that I saw most of my service in France, for just as I had made up my mind that the best way to die was in a cavalry charge, I was promoted and given a commission in the Royal Horse and Field Artillery.

I had expected to be drafted to France the next day but instead I was posted to a reserve battery in Ireland. Here I had six hundred horses, two guns and eight hundred wild Irish Reservists to be equipped and trained for overseas service and taught to ride horses. It was sheer fun for me, for I was in my element. I taught my men to ride in the hunting field with the Muskerry and Duhallow, the nearest packs to my station at Ballincollig. For the moment it was all so enjoyable that we almost forgot the war but the time soon came for me to leave. After passing out eight hundred drivers for France I followed. I was the first temporary officer in the 1st Divisional Artillery of the old Army, for I relieved the first officer casualty in 115 Battery, 25th Brigade.

My battery commander was Ronnie Carrington whose name was a byword as a gunner with the highest possible reputation. When other guns in the first division were rationed to twenty-five rounds per battery per day, he was allowed three thousand rounds on account of his phenomenal marksmanship. 115 was a poker-playing battery but having learnt my lesson on my way to Canada I would excuse myself from 'joining in' and go out into the gun line to spot the flashes from German guns as they were being fired behind their lines. I recorded the angle of these from the gun line so that the air force observers could fly over the next day and give us the range. My services were recognized by the authorities and in due course a Military Cross arrived for me, but Ronnie Carrington did not approve of decorations and said:

"Baker, you don't want to have ribbons all over your bosom, do you? You're out here to kill Germans—that's our job, isn't it?"

And he sent the Cross back to the Brigade Headquarters. When General Fanshawe wrote to the Major inviting me to be his A.D.C., Ronnie, handing the letter to me, impatiently exclaimed:

"You don't want to go and polish the General's buttons for him, do you? Aren't you here to kill Germans?"

So I stayed with my battery while Teddy Schriber, who accepted, was soon promoted rapidly to Brigadier, and later Major-General.

I was fond of General Fanshawe, known to us as "Fanny". He, too, was a crack gunner and keenly interested in what was happening at the Front. Twice a week he would come to my forward observation post and ask me if there was anything new. He had a weakness for strawberries and cream and I used to send my batman to the midnight market at Bethune to secure these delicacies and bring them to me by dawn, when a visit from Fanny was expected. On one of these exciting mornings I happened to mention that a slit in the Church spire of La Bassee would get light and then dark again. My telescope was focused on this slit and the General kept watch. A few minutes later he exclaimed excitedly:

"You're right, Baker, there's obviously an observation post there. Get your guns on to it."

I must admit I felt a bit squeamish about shelling a church and suggested that he should get the heavies on to it. This he did and for two days the heavies kept up fire without hitting the object. The church was just on the other side of the hill and in a fairly safe position. As I was watching at dawn on the third morning there was a terrific explosion and when the rubble and dust cleared from the air the church spire had gone. I told the General this when he came round a few minutes later, and he said:

"What about a spot of leave, Baker? There's going to be a big push soon so I won't suggest more than four days. How about it?"

Of course I accepted.

In London I was invited to a tea-party by some friends all anxious for the latest news from the Front. One old lady who confronted me said:

"Isn't it terrible that those Germans are firing at churches behind our lines?"

I kept very quiet.

On my return to France I was posted to the 39th brigade under the command of Colonel Wardrop—the famous authority on pig-sticking, who had written a book on the subject which had become a classic. The Corps horse show was in the offing and he asked me if I was going to enter. I regretted that I had not a horse fit to enter, and so he very generously invited me to ride his chestnut, a fine upstanding charger. As good fortune would have it I won the Corps Cup on his horse. After this I was given the very responsible job of building a fighting post for the Colonel in preparation for the big push.

In the middle of this job the Germans sent over forty heavy shells in five minutes and twenty-seven of us were buried beneath bricks and mortar and sandbags. The corpses were extracted from the debris and laid in an improvised mortuary. The corporal in charge of the burial party was collecting the identity discs—ripping them off the necks of the corpses. But my identity badge was chained on to my wrist; this had been done during my recent four days' leave. The Corporal gave it a tug and tried to break the steel chain without success. The wrist started bleeding whereupon he called the sergeant and reported:

"This corpse is bleeding."

The sergeant said, "Put it on that old Ford," referring to the van that had brought up the burial tools.

This 'corpse' woke up three and a half days later in the Duchess of Westminster Hospital at Le Touquet, Paris Plage!

Although my body was badly hurt and many bones were broken, I do not remember feeling any pain. It seemed that I myself was outside my body, quite detached from it, watching it with interest yet unconcern. That must have lasted for about three days.

I was haunted by the thought of having taken life. In the fury of the war and in retaliating for the loss of so many of my comrades, quite apart from the destruction by my guns I had taken a heavy toll of German officers from the sniper's post where I would claim my daily turn. In my war madness I used to carve a notch for each 'heart-shot' on an old bow I had found in a shelled chateau, and with glowing pride I had filled it from tip to tip.

A soldier's tribute to his King,
Displayed in every ruddy ring.

In hospital from each notch the eyes of those officers I had killed seemed to look sadly out at me. Their ghostly spectres haunted me, I could not sleep, and my heart came near breaking with regret. Then about four o'clock one morning I thought I saw my former Major, Bob Herman of Cavalry, who had been killed by a stray bullet a few days before, come into my room and stand looking at me from the bottom of my bed. This vision saved my sanity. In order to comfort others I tried to record this impression in the words of a young officer who has been killed and appears to his mother. She has just had news of his death and is

going round her room examining his 'souvenirs'—little bits of
twisted bullet and fragments of shell he had brought her when on
leave from the front. Her heart is seared with grief until he enters
her room.

> *Mother I've come for one brief moment*
> *I must not tarry longer.*
> *Promoted I have been*
> *No longer Earth-bound sorrowing*
> *I pass from sphere to sphere*
> *Carrying new messages of love.*
> *No longer hate I now;*
> *Eyes that once were filled with feud*
> *Now shine bright with gratitude.*
> *Yonder I go to join my comrades.*
> *Regret not the past—*
> *Live in the present—*
> *Crowd each hour with gladness,*
> *Out of the sorrow, out of the sadness*
> *Spring a new world into birth,*
> *Soon strife shall surely cease*
> *And earth with settled peace, break into song.*

He then vanishes as silently as he has come. A great weight is
lifted from his mother as she begins to realize the meaning of life
after death. And so it was with me. Instead of those Germans
being my enemies they became the shining ones, over-flowing with
gratitude for their promotion into heavenly places.

Slowly consciousness returned and I began to recover, though
I still suffered both mental as well as bodily agony as if I were
thawing out after having been frozen. Strangely enough it is not
the freezing that hurts; it is the thawing out which is excruciating.
I wanted to die but with great skill I was dragged back to life and
eventually I returned to the Front, only to be smashed up again.

In the summer of 1917 I was stationed at Swaythling Remount
Depot, near Southampton, and used to receive horses from con-
ditioning depots to take on to France. I made fifty-eight crossings
of the English Channel and conducted eighteen thousand horses,

sometimes as many as four hundred and fifty on a boat, taking them to Le Havre, Dieppe and sometimes in a smaller boat to Rouen. I used to look forward to those summer days on the boat, going up the Seine and being greeted by children lined up along the banks to see the horseboat pass on its way to the Front. It was generally peaceful once we crossed the Channel. Unfortunately, once as we were entering the mouth of the Seine and just as our escort had given his farewell toot and swung round to go out to sea again, she struck a mine, was split in the middle and sank at our stern.

In those Channel crossings I generally contrived to have a blood mare on the top deck just outside my cabin, in case our ship was torpedoed. A horse as a swimming companion in the water is better than a lifebelt, for besides being a friend in distress a clever horse has the instinct to swim towards the nearest land. I would choose a horse with a mane that I could hold on to. When swimming with a horse it is important to keep one's legs as near the surface of the water as possible and away from the horse's feet.

Once, when returning empty, we struck a mine in mid-Channel and the Laskar stokers went on strike, so I ordered my Remount Conducting Party to carry on. They brought the ship into Southampton and I got a D.C.M. for my sergeant.

Soon I had become so fit on this light duty that I was posted to the Remount Depot at Dieppe and used to take horses up the line from there. This was done under cover of night and we usually managed to hand over before dawn and get the horses dispersed to their units before the German planes were up. However, on one of these trips to the Front, a dive-bomber dropped a string on the train which was blown up just as we were shunting back—that was the last time I was smashed up and after the wounds had healed I was fortunate enough to be invited to stay at Lennel, Coldstream, as a guest of Lady Clementine Waring. It was a beautifully wooded property and I was able to help the woodmand and fend for the other officers who had suffered loss of limb.

I was finally invalided out in April 1918. I am deeply appreciative of the skill of the doctors and devoted care of the nurses and sometimes wish that I could arrange a grand reunion of all those to whom I am indebted for my life.

During my convalescence it began to dawn upon me that we were losing more lives through ignorance of health in our great cities than on all Fronts. With Percy Alden of the British Institute of Social Service, I devoted myself to work for the Government, calling upon captains of industry to enlist their help and generally paving the way for the Ministry of Health. It was my earnest endeavour to see that the wonderful war-time sacrifice should not be wasted and that out of it should come a new and saner order of things leading to a lasting peace. As soon as the Ministry of Health came into being I returned to my forestry work at Cambridge.

Chapter 2

CARAVAN VISION

W HEN I investigated the long list of subjects in which I would have to qualify to satisfy the examiners for a Diploma in Forestry, I had the feeling that the life of a simple woodman without the expense and worry of a long tuition in scientific subjects would be better for me, unless there was the possibility of my becoming a leader in my profession. In my blissful ignorance I had imagined that forestry was something to do in a forest, and I had even hoped it was something one learned to make someone else do! But I soon found that to qualify for any of the important Government posts, one had to take Honours in a Science Tripos, and on top of that become proficient in the Principles of Forestry, Principles of Silviculture, Forest Botany, Forest Management, Forest Utilization, Forest Protection, Forest Entomology, and Ecology, as well as fulfil the required conditions for proficiency in Practical Forestry. As far as I could see the only subjects in which we were not required to pass a searching examination were knitting and the care of teething infants! However, the professors were most helpful and they took me by the hands, so to speak, and led me through the technical labyrinth towards the moss and acorns beyond.

Fortunately an early training in Forestry under my father, as well as my experience in the lumber camps of Canada and the nurseries and forests of France, provided exactly the right sort of background for success in my later studies. Nevertheless, I must confess that it was not easy to settle down to the grind again after the war years and with the competition of a new generation of students straight from school.

I was particularly interested in the economic utilization of timber and had made a study of the manufacture and uses of plywood and plastics. Our quest for new uses for timber sometimes led to new industries. In our Forestry School laboratories we carried out delicate experiments with wood fibres and other forest products for manufacturers of paper, rayon, and cellulose. Even as students we were sent to solve knotty problems for industrialists. I was fortunate in having as my lecturer a man with a profound knowledge of wood technology, an enthusiast with a continental reputation. He was none other than Herbert Stone, author of *Timbers of Commerce* and *Wood*. With him I became involved in experiment and invention in the field of the economic utilization of timber. I specialized in Principles of Forestry, Silviculture and Tree Genetics.

Fellow undergraduates in other fields of study had made valuable contributions to scientific invention while still at school, and many of them would migrate to my laboratories in the hope that I would be able to assist them to solve their various problems. In spite of working late at night, I needed only five or at most six hours' sleep and often awakened with creative ideas.

One foggy November morning I dreamed that I saw an aeroplane evolving into a house on wheels. It was quite clear to me where the various parts could be utilized. The great dumps of aircraft material could be put to good use providing homes not only for holiday-makers but for many who were coming out of the forces frustrated in their search for houses.

When I sat down to breakfast, there on the front page of *The Times* was an advertisement from the Government Disposals Board inviting tenders for surplus war aircraft material at Waddon near Croydon. I checked the time of the next train to London, dropped in at the University Typewriting Office and persuaded the Manageress to allow her sister to attend my lectures for that day and take them down in shorthand. By the time I arrived in London I had a rough idea of the types of material, plywood, wings, fuselages and undercarriages I could use in building my house on wheels. It was an experiment, of course, and I was thinking only in terms of one caravan, so I entered the Government Office with some trepidation. When I was asked what I wanted I said, "To begin with, a couple of aeroplane undercarriages."

The man in the office exclaimed, "A couple! This is the Government Disposals Board. That is the smallest lot: thirty-six of them."

Even though they were parked closely to each other they took up quite a big space in the hangar. The tender form in triplicate—

white, pink and yellow—had been placed in my hand, together
with an indelible pencil, and I wrote down the price I would have
given for a pair.

With some impatience, it seemed to me, the clerk inquired,
"What else do you want?"

"Some plywood, please," I answered mildly.

"How much?"

"I should say about 12,000 feet."

"That's the smallest lot," said he, pointing to a stack of beautiful plywood 12 feet long and 4 feet wide, almost touching the top
of the hangar. Again I put down on my tender form the amount I
estimated I would have to pay in the open market for enough for
a couple of caravans. Next I needed ash for the framework and my
guide indicated a huge stack of first-grade 1¼" x 1¼" ash in
lengths of up to 18 feet. Again I made an entry on the tender
form. There were a dozen hydroplane floats in one lot. By this
time I could see my caravan becoming amphibious. There were
bales of holland which I could use for covering the roof and for
making lean-to awnings and auxiliary camping equipment. I could
not resist entering prices for a couple of aero-engines and a stack
of new propellers, struts of sitka spruce from the North-West
Pacific, and a dozen or so ailerons.

I signed the form and a cheque for the amount and apologized
for having detained the good gentleman so long, and caught the
next train back to Cambridge, little thinking that I would hear
more from the thirty minutes I had spent at Waddon.

Ten days later, however, I had a printed postcard from the
station-master at Cambridge, informing me that ten truck-loads of
aircraft material had arrived for me and that I would be charged
demurrage if it were not removed within twenty-four hours!

On the way to my first forestry lecture I paid a flying visit to a
friend whose motor-body building works stood behind the Lion
Hotel, now the main city parking place. I asked if I might be
allowed to put some plywood in an empty shed of his.

"Plywood!" he exclaimed.

"Yes," I said. "Please don't ask me any questions; I am on my
way to a lecture. May I use your telephone?"

"Station Master, will you please deliver the plywood to the

yard of the motor-body building firm at the back of the Lion Hotel? I will give instructions about the rest of the material in about an hour's time."

After my lecture I dropped in at the inn just off Downing Street and said to the proprietor. "Do you mind if I put some aeroplane undercarriages in those open sheds of yours where the farmers put their buggies and carts?"

"Aeroplane undercarriages?" he exclaimed.

"Yes," I said, "thirty-six of them! May I use your telephone?"

"Sorry, no telephone here; there's a kiosk in the street."

"Station-master," said I, "further to my conversation earlier, the aeroplane undercarriages can be delivered to The Jolly Farmer. Yes, and the rest of the ten truckloads of material can be delivered to the first place. If the manager queries it, please say that I will be round later in the afternoon to explain."

By five o'clock that afternoon when I called on my friend again, everything had been delivered. Wtih a piece of charcoal, I designed the first caravan trailer to be mounted on aeroplane undercarriages! I took a clean piece of plywood destined to be part of an aerolongue and first drew the vertical and then the ground-plan of my dream house on wheels.

It had a pullman roof with three pivoting ventilators on each side. It had a low, wide window at the back to allow a through-view for the driver of the towing car. This, together with the side windows, let down in the walls of the caravan like those of a railway carriage. The front door was a double stable-door with upper windows opening out; the lower part of the door was solid, with a spring slot for letters—similar to those used in the front doors of houses.

Over the porch was a little black cat for luck. (It had been given me by a New Zealand girl with whom I was very much in love. I had fondly hoped that I might have persuaded her to marry me, but another New Zealander, a naval commander, had followed her to England, and it was obvious that he too was very fond of her. Forgetting that "all's fair in love and war", I felt that he had a prior claim, although eventually Margot married someone else!) For want of a better name I called my house the 'Navarac'. We were known as

                        N
                        A
                        V
                  CARAVAN
                        R
                        A
                        C
                                          COMPANY
Cablegrams: AVANAVARAC

Until the Navarac appeared on the scene caravans had been
drawn by horses. Being a horse lover myself, I wanted to be able
to take along a couple of horses and saddles for riding.

Soon a dozen or more companies were turning out caravans of
improved patterns—streamlined and much lighter than the Navarac,
which was over 18 cwt. unloaded. Two wheels became the order
of the day, instead of four with turntable.

After all, I was a forester by profession, not an architect or
caravan designer. It was great fun though, and it gave much-needed
employment to aircraftsmen who were finding it difficult to get
work.

And I had now paid my way through Cambridge.

At the completion of my forestry training I applied to the
Colonial Office for the post of Assistant Conservator of Forests in
Kenya. To my bitter disappointment I was turned down on my
medical report. Although I was gradually recovering from my war
injuries, it was a slow process, and the medical standards required
to pass for work on the Equator are very stringent.

I protested to the Colonial Office that I felt fit enough to go
overseas and at once applied for re-examination. As they gave me
little hope, I prepared to set off with one of my caravans to explore
the forests of Europe.

I had planned to cross with the caravan from Southampton in
the usual way, tranship at Le Havre on to a barge and travel up the
Seine as far as I could; then, perhaps on wheels again, across the
country to the Rhine and return that way on another barge down
through Germany and Holland.

Before the war, foresters for India were trained at Coopers Hill,

near Windsor Forest, and they usually went to Germany to gain
experience in preparing Working Plans. The Germans were regarded by the British as the leading foresters in Europe. Early
in their history they had been alerted to the necessity of main-
taining tree cover in high country. When *Alemanni* (meaning
friends) tribes had entered Germany from the south, they had
removed the forest to make farms, with the result that they
came to suffer from serious droughts, accelerated erosion and
desiccation. Some of the Alemanni recognizing the value of
leaving the forest intact, had made only small clearings for the
cultivations which they worked in rotation allowing the trees
to re-establish themselves. This led to a simple form of Forest
Management which was retained through the ages. After Leonardo
da Vinci had evolved the first Principles of Forestry in France,
the Germans had systematized them and with scientific and
mathematical precision had developed schematic silvicultural
systems of an advanced nature. So it was to Germany that generations of forestry students for India went to get their practical
experience.

I had already seen something of forestry at Nancy, the famous
French School of Forestry, and, impressed by the high standard
of training given there, I wanted to enter for an extensive course
of research there before going on to Germany to study their
working plans and management. My view was that there was
little point in taking up a profession unless one had the capacity
and determination to reach the top of the tree. I was determined
to try and learn all I could from the forestry schools and trained
foresters of other countries; so while still at Cambridge I planned
a Continental tour with my NAVARAC.

My work was in the woods or planning forest planting on
moor. Altogether 1918 proved to be quite an eventful year for
me. Besides conceiving the idea of utilizing aircraft material for
the building of caravans, I was busy launching a beekeepers'
club. On my return to Cambridge I had found among the undergraduates many badly disabled people who were no longer able
to take part in vigorous games, among them Blues. It was tragic
to find such people partly paralysed, limping around on sticks
or crutches. One of these Blues had confided in me that for him

life was no longer worth living. He was so depressed I was afraid he might turn on the gas or do something else to end his life.

As a boy of twelve I had started beekeeping, and by the age of sixteen had been the proud owner of sixteen hives. It gave me a good feeling that even while I was studying or working in my father's tree-nurseries my bees would be working for me, hauling in the nectar.

Now that I was confronted with the problem of having to keep these badly wounded people happy while their friends were rowing or engaged in the usual seasonal games, the idea came to me to form an Amateur Beekeepers' Club where such people could learn the ABC of beekeeping.

The 13th Officers' Cadet Battalion at Newmarket was being disbanded; their apiary was advertised for sale. I rode over on my bicycle, saw the apiary and appliances and made an offer to the Adjutant which was accepted. A young widow was kind enough to allow her large orchard to be used to keep the bees.

The Vice-Chancellor of Cambridge, Sir Ernest Shipley, to whom I explained my scheme, willingly consented to be Patron. We had seventeen members, each of whom subscribed a pound and took over a hive. We had a successful season and sold our surplus honey, and at the end of term each member took his hive home, together with a share of the appliances.

While I was at Cambridge, I also joined The Raleigh. In order to qualify for membership one had to have been off the beaten track and to read a paper on the part of the world one had visited. When my turn came I gave an illustrated lecture on North-Western Canada and spoke about the mushroom growth of certain towns, such as Saskatoon.

"When I first went to Saskatoon in 1910," I said, "there were only eleven thousand people. When I left only three and a half years later the population had risen to forty-seven thousand."

In commenting later on the lecture the President remarked that if he had heard aright this was an amazing achievement which should be brought to the attention of the Natural History Society.

Ever afterwards when I met a member of the Raleigh Club I would be asked: "Been back to Saskatoon lately, Baker? What's the population now?"

Chapter 3

THE FIRST MEN OF THE TREES

We advocate that all standing armies everywhere be used for the work of essential reafforestation, in the first instance, in the countries to which they belong, and that each country, as it is able to spare men, shall provide expeditionary forces to co-operate in the greater tasks of Land Reclamation in the Sahara and other deserts.

Green Glory—Forests of the World   R.ST.B.B.

THE GREAT WAR and Cambridge behind, I enlisted on the Green Front in Africa. In November 1920, the call came for me to go to Kenya under the Colonial Office. Just as Richard Baker had drawn me towards Canada, so another pioneer explorer of the Baker clan drew me to my new scene. I had been brought up on the hunting stories of Samuel Baker, who, with Speke, discovered the source of the Nile.

It was in the highlands of Kenya that I came across the nomadic methods of farming which had devastated great tracts of the African Continent. The Romans had created a dust bowl in almost two million square miles of North Africa, wheat mining to satisfy the demands for free bread and circuses! They were followed by wave after wave of Arabs with their goats. These animals kept the natural tree cover from returning and healing the scars made by the Arabs, who had removed the soil-protecting trees with machete and fire. The goats were ready cash for the Arab and they accumulated their wealth in their flocks and herds, driving them before them as they invaded the forest.

It was suggested to me that the nomadic farmers I encountered in the highlands of Kenya were descended from the lost ten tribes, one of which had remained in Ethiopia, the other nine coming south to settle in what to them was their new "Land of Promise". They bartered food for land with the original forest-dwellers—the forest-protectors—the men who lived by the bow instead of the hoe.

Then came the giant steam engines using prodigious quantities of wood. Indian fuel contractors were kept busy felling wide areas of beautiful and valuable trees, such as cedars and olives, and destroying a delectable land that had survived centuries of nomadic farming through crop rotation. Into the cleared land came thousands of white invaders from north and south, from east and west, with tractors and ploughs to hasten destruction with fertilizers and monoculture.

There was but one hope, and that was to restore the indigenous forest. I demarcated a wide area and had it gazetted as a forest reserve. Cultivators were used to clear the rubbish and plant young native trees between the corn and yams so as to leave a potential forest behind them. Thousands of transplants were needed and the departmental grant for reafforestation was negligible.

I enlisted the co-operation of the chiefs and elders of the area through long lecture tours. "What you want," said they, "is an Army of Morans." But these young warriors seemed more interested in dancing than planting trees.

"Trees," they said, "that is *shauri ya mungu*—God's business."

"True," I agreed, "but if all Mungu's parent trees are felled, no young ones will come on."

I found that they had a dance when the beans were planted, and another when the corn was reaped, so I said, "Why not a dance for tree planting?—A Dance of the Trees!"

I explained that, with the help of a committee of twelve chiefs, I would give a prize for the best turned-out warrior and, as their womenfolk could not be left out, a necklace of beads for the most beautiful girl.

Three weeks later, three thousand warriors arrived at my camp, marched past my veranda and fell in before a sacred solitary tree on the hill known as Muguga, a treeless place. (When these warriors cut down the forest to make their farms, they would leave one tree to collect the spirits of all the other trees, so that they should not wander about and be uneasy.)

Through Chief Josiah Njonjo, my righthand man, I called for volunteers, for men who would swear before N'gai, the High God, that they would protect the native forest, plant so many native trees each year and take care of trees everywhere. The volunteers were called the *Watu wa Miti* (Men of the Trees) and were given badges to show this. Then followed the first Dance of the Trees.

A few days later, two men reported that they had lost their badges. Realizing that their badges could be picked up and used by men not bound by their oath, the Head Men—the Forest Guides—decided to adopt a secret sign and a password. They invented a special handshake indicating the threefold promise and the password *"Twahamwe"*, meaning "All as one".

One evening when I returned tired from a long day riding round my forest, my Arab servant, Ramazani bin Omari, told me that many Moran men had gathered to see me. One of them stepped out from the rest and, looking me straight in the eyes, said: *"Bwana*, didn't you tell us that we had to do one good thing every day before the sun went down? In two hours the sun will go down and so far we haven't been able to think of a good deed to do!"

This seemed a direct answer to my need. I had thousands of tiny pencil cedar seedlings—but no money to spend in planting them!

"Come along," I said, "every man who plants out fifty young trees may allow that as his good deed. Then he can go away with a clear conscience, knowing he has fulfilled his obligations."

So evening by evening they came willingly to plant and tend trees when they could not think of a better good deed.

Baden Powell had picked up his scouting in Africa. He had added the 'be prepared' and 'good turn a day' ideas. Now here in the highlands of Kenya a new conception of the Scout Movement had dawned. Tree planting was being used to meet a real need to stop the oncoming desert to the north and the desiccation and erosion that had followed the removal of tree-cover. Tribes who had formerly been hostile or suspicious now vied with each other in tree planting.

The day of the tracker and trapper had passed. Vast areas that had formerly held game had been brought under cultivation; the virgin forest had shrunk to danger-point. In future the man who was rendering the greatest service to his country would be the farmer, forester, the tree-planter.

The Kikuyu and Masai would think nothing of killing a man-eating lion or a leopard that had stolen their goats. To them that would count as a good deed, an act of kindness. Tree-planting came in the same category, perhaps even more so, since nobody who had not fulfilled his tree-planting promise was allowed to be present at a Dance of the Trees.

That was the beginning of what became an important movement for tree-planting in Africa, though all was not plain sailing by any means and I was regarded with some suspicion by certain officials because of the thousands of warriors descending on my camp on Sunday afternoons.

When I went away on local leave to help tree-planting in Tanganyika my *Watu wa Miti* were still coming in the evenings to plant out little trees. At Muguga, in the first big nursery Kenya had seen, they prepared eighty thousand young trees for planting. With the young Mutarakwa cedars they planted olive trees. In the natural forest these two species live next to each other. Pigeons eat the cedar berry but perch in the olive by night. So the cedars spring up around the olive tree, and in turn the olive enjoys the pencil cedar's light shade. Up to this time the main species planted were eucalyptus and wattle, but with the co-operation of young men brought up in the tradition of mixed crops, which they grew perfectly without chemical fertilizers, a varied and impressive nursery was created.

On my return from safari in Tanganyika I was met by Chief Josiah Njonjo, who appeared to be in great distress.

"What is the matter, Chief?" I inquired.

"The farm of the boxes is broken."

My nursery destroyed! I could not believe it—it couldn't be true.

"Bwana, come and see," was the simple reply.

Borrowing my host's pony, I galloped straight to the site of the nurseries. There—where only three weeks ago I had left eighty thousand young trees ready for planting—was a new tennis court! Not a trace of the nursery remained, not a box or a seedling, nothing. I turned away, sickened. All that loving care and voluntary service, all those 'good deeds' wasted! How they must have suffered, those young farmers who had given up valuable time to help to restore their native forest and to bring back the dew and rain to water their vegetable crops. At my prompting they had created a fine nursery, only to have it destroyed by an unimaginative government official.

My superior officer was a puppet who danced to the tune of a régime which had done virtually nothing to protect the soil, forests or wild life. He had studied a little botany, but though I was the first fully-trained silviculturist to be posted to Kenya, he had never been sufficiently interested to come and see my work in this field.

Soon after my arrival I had prepared a forest herbarium, giving the native name of each specimen, which I had sent to Kew for identification. I had also made a collection of timber specimens and sent it to Herbert Stone, Reader in Forestry at Cambridge, to identify and report on as regards economic uses. Besides this I had discovered the secret of germinating the Mutarakwa pencil cedar, the most valuable tree of all. It was to plant these cedars that I had enlisted the services of the volunteers—and now I was pulled up short by the stone wall of officialdom.

As I was wondering how best to help the country but at the time protest, my head of department, Chief Njonjo, who had walked from the station, arrived. Together we gazed at the new tennis court.

"You see what has happened," he said quietly. "Now those young men who came to make the nursery have gone to bush and they will never do another thing for love."

I felt this fine young chief was issuing a challenge.

"Don't talk like that, Chief," I replied. "Those eighty thousand young trees have not been wasted. I am sure they've all been planted well and will help your country another day."

His steady eyes, meeting mine, seemed to gaze into my very heart. He knew, despite my words, that I too was suffering deeply because of the calculated plot to stifle the Men of the Trees.

"You have some good land for nurseries on your territory," I continued. "Now that your men know how to prepare the seed, there is nothing to stop you having your own nurseries." With that we turned away from the distressing sight.

Josiah lost no time in calling his men together. When they had assembled, he said, "*Baba wa Miti* (Father of the Trees) has returned. He says the new white master must have his place to 'knock the rubber about', but we can have our own nursery here on my farm at Kibichiku."

So again they came evening after evening and raised not just eighty thousand, but a million little trees. Other chiefs vied with Josiah to have equally good nurseries. So the dark cloud of the new tennis court had a silver lining, for now the people became more eager than ever to stem the oncoming tide of destruction by planting trees.

In 1923 and 1924 I was in England working in connection with Wembley. I got interested in Nigeria because I was helping with the Timber exhibits from the West Coast of Nigeria and the Gold Coast, as well as in the Kenya Pavilion.

It was in that year that the controversy arose between the white settlers and the Indians in Kenya. The Indians were claiming equality with the British, since they had British passports. There were 22,000 Indians and only 5,000 European settlers. A delegation of the settlers came to London to put the question before the Government. They wanted to get hold of Ramsay MacDonald, then Leader of the Opposition. I was asked if I would approach him on their behalf.

"Well, I shall approach him on behalf of the Africans, you know," I said.

I invited Ramsay MacDonald to lunch with me, but as he was unable to leave the House he asked me to have lunch with him there. He introduced me to a number of people in the Shadow Cabinet.

I said to him: "Mr. MacDonald, I've often wondered why you represent Labour—I shouldn't think you've ever done a day's hard labour in your life!"

"What's that—never done a day's labour in my life?" He looked at me curiously.

"Well," I said, "you know the story of Tolstoy's heaven? You don't? I'll tell you it. Tolstoy always maintained that when a man got to Heaven's gates and asked admittance, St. Peter would demand to see his hands. If they were hard and horny, obviously work-worn hands, he would say: 'Welcome, friend. Enter Paradise.' If on the other hand they were white and soft"—here MacDonald held out his beautiful artistic hands—"Peter would say: 'Go back to earth and do a job of work'!" Here I slapped lightly down on Ramsay MacDonald's hands. It was very unfair of me, I know, but I could not resist the opportunity.

Ramsay MacDonald called over George Lansbury: "Here's a man who says I won't get into Heaven!"

As a result of my subsequent conversation I was invited to give evidence before a special Labour Committee presided over by Colonial Josiah Wedgwood, who was some authority on East Africa. Shastri, who was up at Cambridge with me, and Annie Besant were speaking on behalf of the Indians, and it was soon apparent that the Labour Committee had come under Shastri's spell. He appealed to the emotion of the ideal and talked about the iniquity of the Salt Tax in India. He spoke at length about conditions in Kenya. When he had finished there seemed to be no questions, so I rose and said I should like to ask one question.

"I am sure that we are all deeply impressed with Mr. Shastri's appeal. The only thing I should like to ask is—has Mr. Shastri ever been to Kenya?" I sat down.

The Chairman said impatiently: "Is that all you want to know?"
"Yes."

"Well," turning to Shastri, "you might just answer that."

"Actually, though I have heard a great deal about Kenya, I have never been there."

The whole thing was settled on the lines I suggested. I said that we should not turn over the indigenous African people to anybody, because the British were trustees for the Africans and we must fulfil our trust and not betray them (the Africans) to the Indians or the Europeans. Eventually the question was solved in this way.

My next appointment, in November 1924, was to be Assistant Conservator of Forests in Nigeria. In this post I was fortunate enough to be responsible for the last best forest in tropical Africa. My territory was about the same size as the whole of France and ranged from the Rain Forest through the Orchard Bush to the Savanna types.

It is in the Rain Forest that the great mahoganies vie with each other in their battle for light. Those that attain it are known as the dominating trees. Among these may be found both the black-barked mahogany, the Obobonikwi, and the white-barked, the Obobonufwa.

Here, too, are the tallest of all the mahoganies, the sweet-smelling Entandraphragmas. There are eleven varieties of these handsome trees, yielding some of the most beautiful and useful timber in the world. Rarer and even more strongly aromatic are the Guareas, which produce a darker, attractively grained wood. So much sought after is the Guarea that a single log might fetch £2,000 in the Liverpool timber auctions. They are not gregarious, nor are they to be found in pure stands; an eloquent lesson to those wedded to monoculture in whatever form, in farm or forest.

Each mahogany is surrounded by numerous trees belonging to other families, amongst which is that important family of Leguminoseae—the soil improvers. These I have observed to be good nurse trees for the mahoganies. The more important species of mahogany require the services of a succession of nurse trees throughout their life to bring them to perfection. Some of these provide just sufficient competition to coax the young sapling upwards. Others do their work in secret under the surface of the soil, interlacing the roots, a sort of symbiosis, like the mycelium, which starts as an independent web-like growth, surrounds the sheath of plant rootlets and prepares food that can be assimilated by the growing trees.

The impression one gets in the forest is that there is ruthless struggle going on all the time—a struggle for survival, the strong suppressing the weak. It is almost impossible to follow what is happening in the undergrowth above the ground so tangled are the creepers and woody lianas. But in this zone lies the future destiny of the tree. From the ground it is difficult, if not impossible, to get a clear view of the tree-tops. When I was first stationed in Benin I used to bicycle out before breakfast, first in one direction and then another, hoping to find a point of vantage from which I could study life in the tree-tops. After a couple of weeks I had to own my defeat. But at Sapoba, with the help of a forest dweller I made a ladder and climbed to the top of the tallest tree, where we made a comfortable platform from which I could look out on the whole dazzling life of the tree-tops. It was like being in another world to recognize the crowns of the trees I had known so well on the ground.

How beautiful the whole scene was with tiny birds fluttering from flower to flower, butterflies camouflaged against their feathered enemies! I found myself wondering if the baby mahoganies I had entered on the charts of my quadrats, would ever reach these exalted places. Here the love life of the trees takes place with the tender ministrations of birds, bees and gentle breezes. So little is really known of the romantic world of the tree-tops where the dance of life goes on, fertilisation of flowers takes place and seeds are formed and ripened in the sun's heat. Life in the tree-tops is not all sunshine, for sometimes a storm will break. First an ominous stillness hangs over the scene, broken by a clap of thunder rolling away in the distance, to be followed up by a continuous roar. At the first indication of a storm, I would come down from my look-out tree and retreat to shelter. I sometimes wonder if that tree is still there, or whether it has been felled by a storm or the axes of the timber men. Anyway, I have the deep satisfaction of knowing that in spite of revolutions and counter-revolutions dedicated African forestry officers are guarding their forests and each day are discovering new forest secrets.

"Safari." Say it over again to yourself. "Safari." It sounds full of romance and when you hear it you at once think of Kenya safaris with Armand and Michaela Denis and their amazing films and stories of animals in the wild: leopard, elephant, rhino. They are as much at home in the wilds on safari as in their beautiful place in the country, six miles from Nairobi, where I stayed with them in 1966. Michaela is Vice-President of the Men of the Trees in Kenya and one of the most enthusiastic members. Both she and Armand accompanied me when in the Wakamba Reserve at Machakos we planted 10,000 young trees in ten minutes with the help of 10,000 young people and again three days later when in the Masai Reserve we planted 6,000 little cape chestnut and other native trees in about six minutes with the help of thousands of young people.

Safari simply means 'journey'. It is from the Arabic *safar.* Sahara comes from the Arabic * çahra* (desert). When I hear the word safari, I think of the 25,000-mile journey I made in and around the Sahara in 1964, described in my book, *Sahara Conquest.* It is an exciting thought that by planting trees we can reclaim the deserts, even the great Sahara.

One safari took me to the vast bamboo forests which surround the Aberdare Range roughly in the form of an ellipse with a huge bulge to the north-east. Between 7,500 and 10,000 feet up the bamboo seems to go on and on and on for ever. It does not grow in clumps but is continuous, all the same distance apart like a well-seeded field of grass—giant grass fifty or sixty feet high. This Kenya bamboo is indeed a kind of grass for it is called *Arundinaria alpina*, the grass of the mountains. Each stem is called a culm and has joints or nodes, and each culm is comprised of nodes and inter-nodes. Growth is very rapid and the shoot reaches its full height in about three months, growing about eight inches a day.

My job on this safari was to fell sample plots of bamboo, weigh the culms and discover how many tons of bamboo were produced per acre a year. We thought we would use bamboo for paper-making to save more valuable timber. Besides, our tests showed us that this Kenya bamboo produced a first-class paper which would not only do for wrapping tea and coffee, but for books and writing paper. There were no roads in the bamboo forest so I took thirty-six carriers who fastened their loads with a *mukwa*, a broad rawhide thong which was tied round a load at each end, leaving a loop long enough to reach the top of the forehead of the carrier. The loads rode in the middle of the back and left the arms free to open a passage through the bamboo culms. It was slow going and some-times one had to squeeze oneself between two culms sideways. It was easy to lose oneself and I did! None of my carriers had been here before and they had complete confidence in me. If they had suspected that I had lost my way they might have grounded their loads and left me to my fate, or more likely they would have sat down in despair to await their fate in this bamboo prison from which there seemed little hope of escape. It is difficult for the spoilt children of western civilization to imagine the predicament of a man lost in a vast bamboo forest with not a single solid tree for him to climb to regain his bearings. If only he could shin up a culm and look out on some known feature in the landscape or spot a distant mountain peak, he might regain his lost sense of direction. But if he starts to climb, he will reach less than halfway before the giant stalk begins to waver and bend under his weight, and he slips down or is thrown to earth.

The damp floor of the bamboo forest is no place to sleep, and with little hope of making camp he trudges on till even the dim light fades and soon night closes down on him like a black curtain of despair. It is bad enough to be lost in daylight, but it is much worse when night comes and the unsteady flare of the oil lamp distorts the giant bamboos into grim and fantastic shapes which seem to spring up out of the dark and trap the traveller in a living cage, imprisoning him on all sides. There is always the risk that his trail may have been followed by some hungry leopard or that his scent may disturb an elephant in his mountain home. He is truly in a most difficult predicament.

I was that man who had lost all sense of direction but dared not admit it to my companions. I busied myself examining the culms to see if they had a weather side which would give me a clue as to the direction of the prevailing wind. I found nothing. I lit a fire of dried culms and lay on the damp floor of leaves and sheaths and listened to the silence broken only by the swish of the leaves and creaking sounds which sounded like shrieks from a person being tortured. These gruesome sounds came from interlocked bamboos as they moved in the wind. The story is too long to tell here, but eventually I got out.

My next safari was to the Solai Forest north of Nakuru. I had given myself the job of demarcating a pencil cedar timber concession for a young man who was going to export pencil slats. In this hilly country my line of demarcation went up and down deep gullies and through thick undergrowth. It was here I discovered the secret of preparing the seed to get almost perfect germination and how to grow the trees that are so valuable for timber and for the climate of the Highlands.

The young man who had taken up the timber concession told me once over the dinner-table how his venture had gone. He had sent his pencil slats to a factory in the Lake District, from whom a report had come back that the Kenya Mutarakwa cedar needed special treatment to soften it before it was processed. I remembered that he had shown me the letter at the time when I was Acting Conservator in Nairobi. I had told him that I found no difference between *juniperus virginiana* from America and *juniperus proscera*, our cedar. After that he had gone to the factory himself.

Outside he saw an advertisement for factory hands, so he got into overalls and signed himself on. After a week he satisfied himself that his pencil cedar needed no different treatment from that coming from America. One morning he heard that the Managing Director had arrived. Going to the foreman he requested an interview with him. After presenting his card he was shown into the Managing Director's presence.

"I'm not going to apologize for my overalls or the liberty I have taken in discovering for myself the truth about my slats," he said. "I'm prepared to provide you with so many million slats for the next ten years, and I want you to sign this contract."

When the Director protested that he would have to consult his co-Directors, my friend said, "You sign it at once, or I shall take it over the road to your competitors!"

His story reminded me of the long weeks of research after my discovery about the Mutarakwa cedar. Once I had idly picked up a chip of the wood, and, biting it, had found that it tasted much like the pencils I had chewed at school. When I whittled it there was the same quality of wood which would enable the shaving to break off before the blade reached the lead. I sent samples to Herbert Stone, and his favourable report gave me the confidence to write an article for the Timber Supplement of *The Times* in London. This had created a demand for it and now it had been proved a valuable export. Best of all, I had solved the problem of regenerating it by observing the pigeon's part in dropping cedar berries beside olive trees. With the growing demand for these cedars an ever-increasing supply would be needed. Where the Government had failed the *Watu wa Miti* had stepped in and under Chief Njonjo's leadership his people had succeeded in perpetuating both the cedar and the olive forest.

There were two trains in the station at Nairobi the afternoon I was leaving for England—one going down to Mombasa on the coast and the other going up to Kusumu. I had long wanted to see Samuel Baker's country, for as a boy I had been brought up on stories of his exploration of the Nile. Now the opportunity was given to me.

At Kusumu I took the lake steamer and travelled by way of

Jinja, Lake Kioga and the Sud to Port Masindi where I landed and
went by road to the capital itself, Masindi. It was to be a great day
in the history of that country for, after being exiled to the
Seychelles for thirty-five years, King Kabarega was to be allowed
to return to his own country.

Over two years before, Sir Robert Coryndon, then Governor of
Uganda, had appealed to the Colonial Office at the request of
Dohaga II, reigning King of Bunyoru. Dohaga's plea was: "My
father, the former King, is now an old man and he cannot harm
the British Administration." It had taken the Colonial Office a
long time to reply but in the end they had reluctantly given their
permission for the old King to return—not to the capital but to
Port Masindi and live there, seven miles from the capital.

Although the Colonial Office had not quite forgiven him, the
news that the old King was about to return to his country was the
best news they had had for more than thirty years. Rumours had
gone round that this was to be announced by the Resident when,
in the King's stead, he opened Parliament.

Sir Robert Coryndon had been ashamed of the long delay in the
Colonial Office's reply, and so used me as an excuse for their
tardiness. He decided to make the announcement on the arrival of
a relative of Samuel Baker, King Kabaraga's first English friend,
through whom he had made a treaty with the British Sovereign.

After Samuel Baker had left Bunyoru to continue his exploration, the kingdom had tragically been invaded by ignorant
administrators who did not know the people's customs. They had
violated a secret ceremony and had had to pay the penalty. The
King himself was made the victim of revenge and was banished
from his kingdom.

And now my visit was to mark the announcement of the good
news for which they had been waiting so long. At the time it was
difficult for me to realize the significance of my visit or the deep
diplomacy which had prompted Sir Robert Coryndon's actions.
He had moved on to Kenya to become Governor there just as I
was on the point of leaving. I was his guest of honour at a farewell
dinner at Government House, Nairobi, to which he had invited
representative settlers as well as top Government officials. He and
I were the only two people sitting up at the table, the rest being

under the table, or the weather! (The altitude is frequently blamed
for insobriety!)

I little suspected then that Sir Robert Coryndon was Governor-
General elect for Tanganyika, Kenya and Uganda, and that he had
applied for me to be Chief Conservator of those three territories to
be brought together as United East Africa. Unfortunately during
King George and Queen Elizabeth's visit he died suddenly and the
grand idea had to be abandoned.

But to return to the Kingdom of Bunyoru and the opening of
Parliament in the spring of 1923—I sat on the throne of lion and
leopard skins by the side of King Dohaga II, and listened to the
"Speech from the Throne", so-called although the Resident who
read the King's speech stood at one side. At last the long-expected
announcement was made and the throng surrounding the Parliament
building sent up a mighty shout.

The Court jester, clad in a lion's skin, went through his antics
to the merriment of the spectators. As I looked around at the
faces of the parliamentarians, and under the eaves of the Parliament
building to the huge concourse beyond, I was impressed by the
value of an official jester for parliamentary proceedings. The
Parliament of Bunyoru had preceded the English Parliament by
hundreds of years and once more it was forcibly brought home to
me that other countries had no right to enforce their laws and
customs upon the ancient civilizations of Africa. Samuel Baker
had understood and appreciated King Kabaraga and his Government and in turn had been respected by the King and his people
and treated as the nobleman that he was. I have found that African
royalty, chiefs and elders are sensitive to the people whom they
meet from other countries and expect an aristocracy of mind and
understanding among the people who claim to be their superiors.
Many African rulers are aristocrats in their own right and have
psychic powers denied to us spoilt children of Western civilization.

Parliament having been opened with the announcement of the
return of the old King, Dohaga rose and addressed me, expressing
his gratitude. First he presented me with a pair of leopard's claws
beautifully worked with tiny beads by one of the princesses. As he
handed me this charm he said:

"Honoured friend, this will bring you great good fortune." In

my reply after thanking him I inquired what particular kind of
good fortune it would bring. He promptly replied: "Honoured
friend, you will have many children!"

That day I lunched with the Resident and his wife who greeted
me:

"Baker, I am green with envy. My husband has been here for
fifteen years and he has never been presented with the twin
leopard claws."

She was childless.

Many gifts were showered upon me for my journey, most of
which I had to leave with the Resident.

In the past too often when a forester or administrator has
endeared himself to the people, he has been moved on to another
part of the country or to another colony. I myself had been a
victim of this extraordinarily stupid policy, although in retrospect
it was the finest thing that could have happened to me. When I
took a blow meant for one of my men I burnt my boats so far as
the Colonial Office was concerned but proved myself a friend of
the African in a way that has never been forgotten by the people
or apparently by the Colonial office. The affectionate regard of
millions of my African friends is worth more to me than a dukedom.

If I had stood by while my superior officer felled a Kikuyu to
the ground with the butt end of his hunting crop, I could never
have achieved the work of reclamation and regeneration that I
have been permitted to do in country after country of Africa. To
my dying day I shall carry the memory of the pain of that blow
which could have broken my collar bone. Like King Kabaraga I
was only partially forgiven for what in those bad old days was
regarded as insubordination.

Although I was reappointed by a Labour Government, even so
I was sent as far away as possible from my Kikuyu friends, and I
have never been allowed to enjoy a pension from Kenya or Nigeria.
But I have no regrets at having been deprived of about £35,000,
which I more than earned when I established the Mahogany
Forests of Nigeria on a sustained yield basis, yielding £300,000
worth of timber a year for all time. My discharge from the Colonial
Office liberated me for much greater work in reafforestation and
earth regeneration in other parts of the world. In addition my

influence in forestry in many countries has been demonstrated through the World Forestry Congresses since 1926 and World Forestry Charter Gatherings from 1945 onwards. Through the Men of the Trees, started at my station in the Highlands of Kenya in 1922, tree sense has been created in many countries, and thousands of people have developed a growing appreciation of trees, not only for their timber, but for their beauty and their many indirect benefits to life.

From Masindi I caught the boat for the next stage of my journey down the Nile. The *s.s. Samuel Baker* was then on the Congo but I decided that I would sleep on board for purely sentimental reasons. I changed over to the *Livingstone* at 4 a.m. and sailed on the long journey to Nimule—the next port on the Nile. Walking from Nimule to Rejaff (100 miles) I took the paddle-steamer to Khartoum.

Throughout the journey my serval cat, Ching, was a source of interest and excitement. On board ship when we sailed from Port Said he took a lively interest in the deck tennis, springing into the air and catching the rope rings, much to the astonishment and amusement of the players.

On my arrival in London I immediately took Ching to the Boy Scout Headquarters, to convey a message of greeting from the Forest Scouts of Africa to the Boy Scouts of Great Britain. After being photographed on the roof with the Scouts on duty, I went back to my club. I had no sooner arrived there when there was a message for me. I was wanted on the telephone. It was the Dominions Secretary; he told me that he had sent my message to Marconi House to be broadcast in the weekly Scout Bulletin. (Alfonso Marconi gave the Scouts ten minutes a week for a 'programme'.) The announcer had asked that the man who had written the message be invited to broadcast it, as he felt unable to pronounce the African words in the message. I protested that I knew nothing about broadcasting—in vain. The Dominions Secretary said that it was quite simple and that they would only need to have me there about five minutes before they were due to go on the air.

When I got to Marconi House, I found the set-up quite simple, primitive by today's standards: there was sacking on the walls and a microphone on top of a layer of crêpe rubber on a table. That was all. I swallowed my nervousness and broadcast my message, ending by telling listeners that the mascot of the Forest Scouts and the Men of the Trees in Africa was a tame serval cat called Ching, who sported the green and white of the Men of the Trees. I told them that he was to be seen now in London Zoo. (The following Monday was a Bank Holiday and thousands of Scouts came from all over the country to see Ching.)

After my short broadcast, the Director of Programmes rang me to ask if I would be willing to broadcast on a children's programme he wanted to start up. So for the duration of my stay in England I became 'Uncle Dick' to thousands of children.

On my first night in London I went to the Café Royal to meet my brother, Scott, who was attending a reunion dinner and had promised to join me afterwards. While I was having a coffee with Ching sitting beside me, a corpulent, red-faced man with beery breath came up to Ching breathed heavily over him saying, "Pussy, pussy," and tried to stroke him, whereupon Ching placed a paw firmly on the man's hand. Instead of giving his hand the man drew it away rapidly and got a slight scratch. I apologized but told the man it was his own fault as he should have left my kitten alone when told to do so. He retorted, "I know all about these things— I've hunted big game in Africa."

Just then my brother joined me and we left for my club.

A couple of days later a letter arrived from a lawyer in the City, saying:

"We are writing to you on behalf of our client, a well-known trainer of horses, who on the night of the 10th was savagely attacked and bitten by your wild animal. He is now suffering from rabies and will have to go to Paris for a Pasteur cure. What do you intend to do about it?

I replied:

"Dear Sir,—I acknowledge your letter and am sorry that your client has been hurt. At the same time I admit no responsibility. Incidentally, it was a cat and not a dog, and

a scratch and not a bite, and so he cannot be suffering from rabies. I think the enclosed will meet the case.
                                    Yours, etc."

I had bought a small tin of Zam-Buck from Perkins, the chemist in Piccadilly. I wrapped the little tin of green ointment in tissue paper, slipped it into the envelope and posted it.

The following day I went off to Wiesbaden to join my younger brother, Tom, who had married an Austrian, a famous tennis player and linguist. I was wanting to get up to date with my forestry work and was also glad to have the opportunity of taking the hot baths as I was still suffering from old war injuries. In many ways the war still seemed to be on. The occupation armies, both British and French, were there. The mines were at a standstill and food in the unoccupied territory was very scarce. Long queues of women could be seen waiting from the early morning hours for a little bit of butter substitute or a few potatoes. The value of the mark had sunk so low that people living on an annuity would sell it and spend the proceeds on the barest necessities of life in the course of a few days. There were two old ladies who had sold their house and in the course of a couple of weeks had exhausted their capital. They sold all their furniture and clothes, keeping one dress which they took turns to wear when they went out to buy a crust of bread. Some days later they were found in their room, dead. They had turned on the gas. Retired colonels, having been forced to part with their houses and belongings, would fill a rucksack with what they had left and go off into the forest to eat berries and nuts and exist as long as they could.

I went to the dentist to have a tooth filled. The fee was 250,000 marks. I begged the dentist to take double that amount, which would only have been fivepence in English currency, but he refused, saying that this would be unprofessional.

On my return to London I found a summons waiting for me at the Club, "Smith versus Baker and the Café Royal, jointly and alternatively £75 and costs". The case was heard in the Westminster County Court and went on for three days while learned counsel argued about the domesticity of the creature. On the third day, the Café Royal agreed to settle and left me to fight alone. The

evening papers were full of pictures and varying headlines, "Wild
Cat attacks man in well-known West End Café", etc. A wonderful
advertisement for the Café Royal but not the sort of publicity
that a junior forest officer would be encouraged to seek!

On the following day the prosecution counsel subpoenaed the
cat from the Zoo and, when I had given my evidence, addressed
the judge.

"Your Honour, you've heard how the defendant has said what a
nice, quiet, little beastie he is, how he has slept on his bed at night
and played with children. And so, I've brought this wild creature
from the Zoo. What is a Zoo for, your Honour, but for wild
animals? Keeper, bring the cage."

The keeper stepped forward with a smallish box.

"Keeper, open the cage."

Ching emerged cautiously, stretching his legs, for he had been in
a cramped position. He gazed round the court, mystified. I called,
"Ching!"

When he made a dive towards me he was roughly pulled back
whereupon he attacked the keeper's legs, biting and tearing his
trousers.

The counsel continued, "Now, Your Honour, just stroke the
nice little beastie."

"God forbid," said the judge. There and then he gave his verdict
against me for the full amount unless I agreed to settle, which I
did on the advice of my counsel.

Ching had become famous overnight. Mascots of him were being
sold in Bond Street. For some time it was a smart thing for ladies
to wear a replica of him on their lapel or hat. As long as I was in
England I visited him on Sunday afternoons, taking him out for a
walk on a lead, and he lived longer than any other serval cat in
captivity.

Chapter 4

I DISCOVER SOME FOREST SECRETS

Whoso walketh in solitude,
And inhabiteth the wood,
Choosing light, wave, rock and bird,
Before the money-loving herd,
Unto that forester shall pass
From these companions, power and grace.
Woodnotes. EMERSON

I LEARNED EARLY to regard the forest as a society of living things, the greatest of which is the tree. Its value depends upon its permanence, its capacity to renew itself, to store water, its many biological functions including that of providing Nature's most valuable ground cover, and building up to a great height stores of one of the most adaptable of raw materials: wood.

We stand in awe and wonder at the beauty of a single tree. Tall and graceful it stands, yet robust and sinewy with spreading arms decked with foliage that changes through the seasons, hour by hour, moment by moment as shadows pass or sunshine dapples the leaves. How much more deeply are we moved as we begin to appreciate the combined operations of the assembly of trees we call a forest.

As long as a soil is covered with forest, its humus is maintained. The basic forest problem lies in its composition and regeneration. In the forest the processes of decay and growth always balance one another. The vegetable wastes together with the by-products of the animal population form a mixture on the forest floor. As we examine this mixture from time to time we find it remains practically constant in depth, in spite of annual additions from leaf-fall that take place. This mixture is drawn upon at an even rate by earthworms, fungi and bacteria, and the resulting humus in turn is absorbed by the soil and provides the trees and undergrowth with the food materials they require. Thus the forest manures itself and with the help of the earthworms and other animals distributes this manure through the upper layers of the soil. Everything is done by Nature quietly and efficiently. No artificial fertilizers, no selective weed-killers, no pesticides and no machinery are needed in the household of the natural forest.

In that vast evergreen forest Nature works in perfect rhythm; roots digging deep or exploring nearer the surface for food and moisture. Imperceptibly Nature builds those mighty pillars with aisles innumerable, arches multiplex, in the cathedral of the forest.

A teeming life goes on in the forest without any of the problems that confront mankind in similar circumstances. There are no dust-bins to empty, no water-borne sewage, no town clerks or city councillors or armies of officials, with more and more rates to pay, no ever-growing burden of debt.

The forest solves its own sanitary problems by direct action while man evades them. The forest has been described as the perfect sanitarian, the supreme chemist. In its economy it perfectly combines Capitalism, Communism and Social Credit and instead of building up a burden of debt it stores up real wealth—the wealth of the woods. As Henry van Dyke so aptly put it:

> In the wealth of the woods since the world began
> The trees have offered their gifts to man.

In the mahogany forests I saw to it that the soil was never exposed to direct sun, rain or wind. The rain was broken up by the canopy into fine spray; the ground was permeable; the soil below readily drank in the rainfall. I carefully avoided anything in the nature of weeding or unnecessary cultivation. Vast quantities of water from the rain-storm and the river are held up in transit by the thick carpet of permeable humus. In this way my forest acted as a huge reservoir only gradually releasing the water in the form of springs into the clear, deep, slow-flowing Jamieson River.

I had been somewhat concerned that although I was issuing permits to fell up to £25,000-worth a month little was being done to perpetuate future supplies of this most valuable species by encouraging natural regeneration of the desired mahoganies by silvicultural operations. For years the forestry department had been issuing permits to fell, but so far the Science of Forestry had not been applied. My first official letter to the Director of Forests asked for two extra forestry officers as I claimed that much valuable revenue was being lost through lack of proper supervision in the forest.

Ten days later I asked that I might spend half the revenue I was collecting in planting up or regenerating cut-over areas so that the forest might be worked on a sustained yield basis, to which I had a prompt reply to the effect that as I was already understaffed the Director was unable to grant my request since there would not be proper supervision in the spending thereof!

Here I was, a fully trained silviculturist, issuing permits to fell tens of thousands of pounds worth of mahogany with a mere pittance of £100 a year to spend on reafforestation. It had been a long and arduous struggle to qualify for the important position I was holding, yet now I had to battle with the authorities to be permitted to do that very job. In the end, however, I made a case for sound silvicultural management and was able to introduce various systems to ensure natural regeneration of the mahoganies. This involved the removal of so-called Secondary Species and if my management was to be economically as well as silviculturally successful I must find a market for them. It was then that I decided I would make a collection of all the secondary timbers, take samples to England and examine them anatomically and microscopically to arrive at their highest possible utilization.

In 1926 I arrived at the Imperial Forestry School at Oxford, prepared to devote as much time as possible to investigating the best uses for these secondary species. If only I could succeed it would justify my silvicultural systems and ensure wealth from these great mahogany forests for all time. For three years I had been working and planning for the First World Forestry Congress to be held in Rome and now the time of its inauguration was drawing near. I was to represent Nigeria there—this had fitted in with Professor Troup's plans for me and I arrived at Oxford just as he was ready to set out for Rome accompanied by Lord Lovatt, Chairman of the Forestry Commission, and Robinson the Secretary. Everything fitted in perfectly.

It had long been my ambition to return by way of Kenya and have a reunion with the original Men of the Trees. On my previous leave I had been present when the African Society presented Maréchal Lyautey with its Gold Medal. In his presentation speech the President, Lord Buxton, had mentioned that it was the first time a foreigner had received this distinction, to which the Maréchal replied, "Please do not call me a stranger for I am a fellow colonial. Any success I have achieved I attribute to what I have learnt from your great administrator, Governor Louard of Nigeria." I was among the guests presented to the Prince of Wales. He recalled our soldiering together in the First Divisional Artillery in France. I invited him to be President of the Men of the Trees and he said, "Ask me again when I return from Kenya next year." My leave was to coincide with his visit and I had been looking forward to turning out to greet him with some thousands of the members of the Men of the Trees under the sacred Mugumu tree where the first volunteers had pledged themselves to plant trees and protect forests.

I had often spoken to the *Watu wa Miti* of this princely humanitarian who was always ready to lend a helping hand to the poor and under-privileged. Thousands had seen and admired his portrait which I carried with me on safari and a vast concourse of Men of the Trees would have turned out to welcome him to Muguga.

It was not to be. Towards the end of my tour I received a favourable report of my silvicultural experiments at Sapoba and was instructed to hand over fully to an officer who had just returned from studying tropical silviculture in India and proceed to new territory two hundred and fifty miles north to initiate similar silvicultural experiments there. This was a great disappointment to me as I had gone to the expense of providing for petrol at different stages on the journey and had sent messages ahead to pave the way for a rally of the old members to welcome the Prince.

In retrospect I cannot but feel how important that gathering would have been in the formative period of the Men of the Trees. Great as their contribution has been to Africa, far more might have been achieved if I had been permitted to return before tensions between the indigenous peoples and the settlers had been allowed to develop. Indeed, years of unease, strife and bloodshed might have been prevented, had not the exigencies of the service prevented my meeting with the Prince and my Men of the Trees. It is a significant fact that my district was the only one in Kenya where the peace was kept through the turbulent years of the emergency and that my interpreter at the first Dance of the Trees, Chief Josiah Njonjo, was the only Kikuyu Chief not shot by the British or murdered by the Mau Mau.

But fate seemed to be against my returning to Kenya and on my arrival at my new station the people hid in the bush. Perhaps they had been shot over and frightened. Fortunately I was able to allay their fears and with the help of one of my boys who understood their language enrolled a number of forest workers whom I set to work laying out new nurseries.

In levelling the land I thought it would be useful to have a couple of wheelbarrows and ordered these from railhead, sending two men to fetch them thirty miles away. The following day they returned with the wheelbarrows balanced on their heads! They had not yet discovered the use of the wheel. This was confirmed later when I told them to fill the barrows with earth; they put in a little, then stopped, protesting that it would be too heavy to lift. However, I persuaded them to fill it and proceeded to demonstrate by running a loaded barrow along a plank. I selected the strongest-looking man in the gang and asked him to try. He took two steps forward and fell over with the load which emptied itself on one side of the plank. It was amusing to initiate them into the use of the wheel and very soon they discovered the knack of balancing the load and running along the plank, although not before they had spent much time laughing at themselves for being unable to imitate me.

All went well until I got a bad bout of malaria and that same night there was a tropical downpour. The building contractor had sited my hut in a dried river-bed and in the middle of the night I woke with a temperature of 105° to find loads of equipment floating around my bed! With the help of a boy I climbed the bank to my little Morris Cowley and, almost blind with fever, drove myself 120 miles to Lagos. There it was decided to put me on the next boat to England.

In my new station I had missed the friendly help of my old

interpreter, Igabon, who had remained in Benin. A few months before he had been very seriously ill and the day came when the doctor told me that the only hope was to operate. He intended to do this that evening on his return to the station. I found poor Igabon in great suffering; he indicated to me where the pain was worst. I took my ring with a Persian stone and, making the sign of the Cross over the area, gave him the ring to hold. By the evening when the doctor returned he decided not to operate. Igabon had apparently made a successful recovery. Yet the day that my ship sailed from Lagos, he died. He had depended so much on my presence, it seemed, that when the hawser dropped into the water that invisible thread was broken. For my part I felt like death and would have been quite willing to die but for a cheerful Irish ship's surgeon who jollied me along and would not leave me to myself. Three days out from Lagos, at the end of the Bight of Benin, is a place known as the "Graveyard" as so many had succumbed to the sudden change of temperature. There is a saying among old sea captains about the Bight of Benin—"Few come out tho' many go in." I was one of the lucky ones.

Upon arrival in London I reported at the Colonial Office, assuring them that I was ready to return to Nigeria at the end of my leave. In the meantime I had been invited to Palestine by the Governor designate, Sir John Chancellor, to assist him in launching a progressive planting plan.

Sir John had lectured to the Royal Geographical Society in Edinburgh and given them an account of his visit to Kenya, which he had visited on his return from Rhodesia where he had been Governor. He spoke of his excitement at seeing a wide expanse of newly planted indigenous trees at Muguga, seventeen miles from the capital city. On visiting the headquarters of the forestry department Sir John had asked what their planting allowance was and had been informed that it was negligible—a mere £500 a year. Said they:

"Of course we've got our natives very well trained."

He congratulated the Chief Conservator on his fine achievement, who explained that all this work had been done voluntarily by the natives. Sir John had expressed surprise that such extensive work had been voluntarily undertaken and asked if this had anything to do with the Men of the Trees. The Forest Officer admitted that I had been Assistant Conservator of Forests in this area and Sir John enlarged upon this in his lecture.

That night he stayed with the President, Lord Salvesen, who told Sir John that I was staying with his family at Mandal in Norway and that he would be seeing me the following Tuesday.

"I wonder if you would be so kind as to give him a message," said Sir John. "Next week I shall be leaving for Palestine to take up my post as High Commissioner and I'm anxious to meet him before I leave. All my dinners and luncheons are official engagements but I should be pleased if he would have breakfast with me any morning as I want to get his formula. He was so successful in uniting warring tribesmen in his cause of tree-planting I want to enlist his help in uniting warring religionists."

On Tuesday, on his arrival at Mandal, Lord Salvesen gave me the message and the following Friday I had breakfast with Sir John in London. He invited me to stay with him in Jerusalem and start a branch of the Men of the Trees there.

I protested that I had been invalided from Africa without a pension and that it would be difficult for me to accept his invitation. He suggested that I should ask my friend Lord Salvesen to arrange for a passage on one of the Salvesen boats and I would be his guest from Kantara onwards. Everything went to plan and I was met by the A.D.C. at Jerusalem. After lunch I asked Sir John if I might go to Mount Carmel to pay my respects to Shoghi Effendi, guardian of the Baha'i Cause.

"Of course," said Sir John. "Take my car—my chauffeur will drive you. But don't be late for dinner. I've asked the grandees to meet you."

At the Persian Colony of Mount Carmel Shoghi Effendi himself greeted me and handed me an envelope which contained his application for life membership of the Men of the Trees. He promised that he would do much more than this and that I would succeed in bringing all the Heads of Religion in Palestine together in the cause of the trees.

The dinner in Jerusalem that night laid the foundation of my mission to Palestine. The following morning, with the approval of the High Commissioner, I called on the Grand Mufti, President of the Supreme Moslem Council, who agreed to meet the High Commissioner three weeks later at the American Colony to discuss the problems of large-scale reafforestation in the Holy Land. From him I went to the Latin Patriarch and said that the High Commissioner had been impressed by the planting of trees around their monasteries. Would he be prepared to meet the High Commissioner and myself and confer with us on the question of re-treeing the land? He accepted. Then I went to the Chancellor of the Hebrew University, on to the Greek Orthodox Patriarch, and finally to the Bishop of Jerusalem and the Near East, giving each the same invitation though I did not mention that I had spoken to any of the others.

I had already enlisted the co-operation of heads of government departments and the Chief Forest Officer. I then prepared my speech and gave it to the printers for transcription into Arabic, Hebrew and English in time for the gathering at the American Colony.

The next three weeks I devoted to filming Sir Flinders Petrie's dig at Tel Farah, one of the uttermost cities of Judah. Unbeknown to him his secretary had coaxed me to film each complex as it was opened up. Sir Flinders had identified the Tel as Tel Farah, meaning hill of escape, with Beth Pellet, house of escape. This had been the fortress of David's famous Pelltite guard and here Sir Flinders had found bronze weapons which were among the first to be used.

At the top of the Tel were remains of Allenby's trenches where souvenirs of the Great War were found, such as copies of *The Tatler* still intact, spurs of cavalrymen, identity discs, mess tins, and knives and forks. Under the trenches was a Roman city with a pillared hall and baths; there was even a lavatory where water had been laid on. Under the Roman city was one from the Greek period, which had been damaged by grain pits from the Roman period. As each complex opened up the finds became more exciting.

Then a city of Shishack was unearthed. It was protected by a great wall and it was here that I lay in wait for Sir Flinders Petrie, the Father of Archæology, who hated the idea of having himself or his excavations filmed. I built a blind, planting a newly excavated basket of potsherds at a strategic point inside the wall. I did not have to wait long. Soon he emerged through a slit in the great wall and was at once attracted to the latest finds which I had planted. He quickly turned them over and, picking out those that interested him most, slipped them into his pocket, proceeding on his way to inspect his workers while my telephoto camera followed him into the distance. Finally Sir Flinders removed the sand which had filled the deep trench in the fortress of the Shepherd Kings. When Allenby inspected this ancient fortress he expressed the view that in those days it would have been impregnable.

Simultaneous with the archæological excavations on the Tel, graveyards of those periods were being discovered and precious finds being unearthed by Arab workers. The tallest of these was Abdel Magid and his constant helper was a girl by the name of Delilah. Like Samson's Delilah, she came from Gaza and she too lived up to the Delilah reputation which Abdel found very upsetting!

Sir Flinders' key to dating the finds and various sites was pottery, for pottery fashions changed almost every year. It was seldom traded owing to its fragility yet was indestructible, being easily put together. Scarabs were a further key to dating the finds. During my three weeks at Tel Farah I slept on a camp bed in the skullery where skulls from the graves were stored on shelves, and under my blanket I struggled with my four-hundred-foot reels of film, testing strips to make sure that my camera was behaving. This was my first introduction to archæology in the field and it was a privilege to live among Arabs who had hardly changed their way of life since Bible times. Our finds were confirming the story of the past and making the sacred writings live again, not only for me but for those who saw my films and read my articles in *The Times*.

I returned to Jerusalem the day before the gathering and lost no time in contacting the heads of government departments to make sure that each of them would be there to assist me in welcoming the prominent religious leaders.

It was with some trepidation that I welcomed the Grand Mufti the following afternoon. I introduced him to Colonel Bowman, Director of Education, who was a brilliant Arabic scholar. I had had the hall prepared with curtains on one side forming cubicles with just two seats in each. Into the seclusion of one of these, Colonel Bowman led his charge. Next to arrive was the Latin Patriarch for whom I had a good Catholic waiting. Next came the Chancellor of the Hebrew University and I entrusted him to Mr. Abrahams, Minister of Lands, and so on, each of the Grandees being escorted into a cubicle to await the signal of the arrival of the High Commissioner. In the meantime the centre of the hall was quickly filled with other guests, including officials and administrators of the various departments of government. The High Commissioner arrived punctually and immediately the meeting came to order, the heads of the religions taking their reserved seats in the main body of the hall. Sir John gave a brief introduction.

"Your Excellencies, Ladies and Gentleman, there is really no need for me to introduce our speaker to you this afternoon. As you already know him I will ask him to address us."

I rose to address this distinguished gathering, fully conscious of my great responsibility. We were making history: this was the first time that the heads of all these religions had been brought together. I told them that there was no land needing trees more than Palestine and that no land would respond so well to planting. The land had suffered for centuries from invading armies. Olive trees had been taxed and to avoid taxation the farmers had cut them down and used them for fuel. I reminded them that in historic times the country had been well wooded. For the future prosperity of the country tree-cover must be restored to the hills.

Then I called upon them all to assist me in founding the Men of the Trees in Palestine. I drew their attention to the sheets in their hands on which I had indicated that the High Commissioner had kindly consented to be Patron and invited the heads of the religions to be the Vice-Patrons.

"I have taken the liberty," I said, "of including your Excellencies' names. The heads of government departments have kindly consented to act on my Executive and the Chief Forest Officer has agreed to be secretary/treasurer. I trust you will allow your names to stand as printed."

My proposal was then put to the gathering and carried unanimously. I promised to donate £1,000 to help start nurseries and the High Commissioner promised a further £1,000. Very soon forty-two nurseries were established.

A few days later I took part in a tree-planting ceremony at Biet Vegan—the house and garden suburb of Jerusalem—four miles from the Holy City. Four thousand school children marched from Jerusalem with their parents, uncles, aunts and teachers. I stood with the Rabbi of that quarter by the Arch of Welcome inscribed in Hebrew, "Welcome to the Young Planters", welcoming each contingent as it arrived at the Arch. The head of the four-mile-long procession was arriving at the Arch of Welcome just as the last contingent was leaving the city. There were four hundred trees in place and ten children to assist in planting each tree under the instruction of their elders. When the four hundred roadside trees were duly planted and watered, the children were each given a bag of fruit and nuts with a bottle of fresh orange juice. They settled on the side of a sunny hill overlooking the scene of their planting. This revival of the Feast of the Trees took place on the 15th of Shebat, 1929. During the long years of the Dispersion, Jews had kept this memorable feast established in Levitical times by eating fifteen different kinds of fruits grown in the Holy Land. Now with the return to the Land they were once more planting in memory of the ancient saying, "He who plants in the land shall possess the land."

Field-Marshal Viscount Allenby had been my strong supporter in this, for even before the end of the war in Palestine he had enlisted Arab villagers and had them planting fast-growing eucalyptus in the mountain sides. Back in London he welcomed me at his home in Wetherby Gardens and signed a letter I had drafted to the Editor of *The Times* making an appeal to cover the cost of the establishment of the tree nurseries and roadside planting in Palestine. Lord Melchett and Sir Francis Younghusband also signed the letter, which brought in £850 in the first week. I was able to raise this to £1,500 as a result of my next lecture tour in the U.S.A. and Canada.

The funds thus raised were drawn upon to plant the new forest between Jerusalem and Jaffa. The High Commissioner saw to it that a plaque inscribed in Arabic, English and Hebrew was put up, indicating that this was the forest of the Men of the Trees. Years afterwards, when I was entertained at the Garden Club in London by a member, I was introduced to her son who was in command of a company which for three days had endeavoured to catch up with Arab marauders. At the end of that time they emerged, tired and hungry, their emergency rations finished, and the Arabs still hiding in this forest. The officers reported their failure to their Colonel who in turn reported to the General, who called on the Governor, General Wauchope, to suggest that the forest be cut down so that the army could complete their job.

"What, General!" said the Governor. "You must not dare to touch a tree—those were planted by the Men of the Trees—it's as much as my job's worth!"

Some years later in London, when I arrived at my Club from overseas, Ferguson, the hall porter who had known me since 1916, said, "General Wauchope was inquiring for you."

In the course of my conversation with the General I asked him if there were any truth in the story of his wanting to cut down the trees and being warned off on the grounds that he would lose his job. He replied, "That's true, or near enough. You'd have had me sacked, Baker, wouldn't you?"

Before returning to England from Palestine I was invited to give a lecture to the Arabs at Acre. My subject was "Some Economic Aspects of Re-afforestation." At the conclusion an old Arab stood up to propose a vote of thanks.

"Sir, I'm not going to make a speech but I want to tell you a story. It's one that was told me by an old Persian friend, Abbas Effendi: A king was out walking once when he came upon an old man planting olive trees. The king said, 'You're a very old man to be planting olive trees; what profit will you get from your planting?' And the old man replied, 'Others planted that I might eat—I plant that others may eat.' The king was so pleased with him that he turned to his servant, saying, 'Give him a bag of money.' Whereupon the old man held up the bag of money and said, 'You see, your Majesty, my planting has already brought me profit!' The king again turned to his servant and said, 'Give him another bag of money.'

"It will be a long time before we see the results of the planting we shall certainly do as a result of your good advice this day but we feel you have already given us two bags of money—thank you."

Chapter 5

BATTLE TO SAVE THE REDWOODS—
EARTH'S OLDEST LIVING TREES

*. . . they seem to be forms of immortality standing here
among the transitory shapes of time.*

EDWIN MARKHAM

EVERYTHING WAS drawing me westwards. Through the kindness
of the Managing Director of the Canadian Pacific I was given
a free passage on one of their empty boats going out to New
York for the winter shuttle-service to Bermuda. And so I set out
on a tour of the world's forests with little more than a fiver and a
free ticket to New York, only this time with my Palestinian films
and slides illustrating "The Adventures of a Forester in Kenya and
in the Mahogany Forests of Nigeria." It was a serious blow to me
when the customs officer charged duty on my film, leaving me
with less than five dollars. I put up at a modest hotel in Grammercy
Park, confident that I would be able to get articles commissioned.
I spent the next morning ringing up editor after editor and drew a
complete blank. Towards noon I decided to take a walk in the
park. A few steps from my hotel door I bumped into an old friend
from Kenya, Major Radcliffe Dugmore, who had produced one of
the finest big game films, *The Wonderland of Big Game*.

He was visiting New York on serious business. Some film producer had pirated one of the most spectacular scenes from his
film and the Major had come to New York to collect his dues or
take legal action. Having been with him in Kenya I could identify
his shots.

I soon found that Dugmore was very popular among the members of his club, the Players. We were invited to the high table with
the committee where, after swapping news, we drifted into general
conversation. I related how an American doctor on board ship had
boasted to me, "Say, Baker, you may think that in England you
have a good health service, but right here in this city, believe me,

we have the biggest and best lunatic asylums in the world." I had laughed—"That's too funny"—at which he had repeated, "I said we had bigger and better lunatic asylums than anywhere in the world." "That's just why I laughed," I had said, "as if what you said were something to be proud of. Among the forest dwellers of Africa I've never found a lunatic; cut off from the rest of the world they have evolved a social system, a moral code suited to their environment and they live their carefree lives in the forest without the gadgets of modern civilization. Unlike the West, they do not destroy their habitat." After describing some adventures I had had with the mighty bowmen I thanked my host and excused myself as I had another appointment. As I rose from the table a member of the group followed me.

"Excuse me, have you got a minute to spare?"

"Yes, I've got two, I've got ten."

"Have you ever written a book?" he asked.

"No, not a proper one, though I have contributed scientific articles to journals and written a number of stories for magazines on my life as a forester."

"Well," he said, "if you can write as well as you talk, you ought to be able to write an exciting book. We are the Dial Press of New York and we reckon that we publish the best travel books in this little city. Come round and meet my partner."

He pushed me into a taxi and a few blocks away a lift took us to the top of a tall building where I was introduced to his partner, Lincoln McVeigh.

"I want you to meet Baker. I've been listening to a most interesting story and I tell him he ought to write a book for us."

McVeigh said, "Will you?"

"How long?" I asked.

"Seventy-five thousand words," said he.

"Illustrated?" I held out a number of glossy prints for his perusal. "How many?"

He suggested a hundred.

"Now," I said, "I want to make a special request. So many books are ruined by putting two or more pictures on a page. I would like a clear page for each picture."

"I agree," said McVeigh. "We shall only need forty-eight, but let us have a hundred to choose from. When can you let us have the manuscript?"

"In a month's time."

"Are you sure that is giving yourself time? We will put five weeks in the contract which gives you a week's grace. It's the usual form—if you don't like the look of it, ring us in the morning."

"There's just one more request I would like to make. You see I shall have to get down to this, take on stenographers and pay for the enlargements. Would you be good enough to let me have, say, five hundred dollars on signing the contract, and five hundred on delivering the manuscript?"

"Certainly," said McVeigh. "I will have a clause added to that effect. Good-bye and good luck."

I lost no time in getting on with the book. I returned to my diminutive room, having enlisted the help of the secretary of an attorney I had met at the Club. I dictated from four to eight and at eight o'clock she was relieved by Dr. Bestor's secretary who had promised to work till midnight. At eight the next morning, I started with a stenographer I had obtained from an agency. At midnight I went into the Players' Club and enjoyed my one meal of the day.

In ten days I had finished dictating my first manuscript—*Men of the Trees*. I took another week to number the pages and caption the photographs and delivered the finished manuscript and collected my second five hundred dollars.

"Who would you like to write the foreword?" asked the publisher.

I suggested Dr. Bestor of the Chautauqua Institute but he said, "Think again." I then suggested the President of the Bank of America. But he said, "Think again."

"I can't," I replied. "You think."

"Do you know Lowell Thomas, broadcaster and author of *Lawrence and the Arabs*? Would you mind my asking him?"

"I should be happy indeed," I replied.

When I went to thank Lowell for his generous foreword he said, "I've followed your work ever since the first Dance of the Trees in Africa. I always call you the Lawrence of Africa because you have done for the African people what Lawrence did for the Arabs. Tell me, how do you say 'Good-day' in your language?"

"*Jambo*," I replied.

"How do you say, 'Good-bye'?"

"*Kwaheri*."

"Write it down," he said.

So I wrote it down.

"*Kwaheri*," he repeated. "I wish to God I was coming with you on this world trip. I'm going to tell the world about this. Keep in touch with me."

The following night I lectured to a packed audience at the Carnegie Museum, Pittsburgh, on "The Adventures of a Forester." At the close an old lady of nearly ninety came up to me and said, "You remind me of my grandfather. He spoke King's English, or was it Queen's English in those days? I knew you were going to talk about trees and so I copied out a beautiful little tree poem by our great tree poet, Joyce Kylmer, who was killed in the war; it is called *Trees*."

"Thank you, Madam. That is most kind of you."

The queue of people waiting to shake hands stretched away to the middle of the hall. The next person pumped my hand appreciatively with her right and with her left presented me with an illuminated poem.

"It's *Trees*," she said. "I did it for you. It is a poem by Joyce Kylmer, our famous tree poet."

"Thank you, Madam. How kind of you. I shall treasure it." It seemed that every other person was thrusting those beautiful lines upon me! Anyway, this first public lecture in Pittsburgh could be described as a success.

That night Lowell Thomas had started his *World News* with:

"*Jambo!* everybody, *jambo!* I've just been having a lesson in Ki-Swahili from the Man of the Trees, you know, that fellow Baker who started the Dance in the Trees in Africa. I'm going to tell you all about it and how he enlisted the warring tribesmen of Africa in his Men of the Trees and soon had them planting millions of them."

Lowell Thomas went on with news about Europe and India and ended up: "*Kwaheri!*—Goodbye. You see I have learnt my lesson very well; but we will not say goodbye to the Man of the Trees— we have got to watch this fellow. He is just off to the redwoods in California and on to New Zealand and Australia. By the way, he has written a book which will be out in the fall. It is called *Men of the Trees. Kwaheri.*"

I understood then why the Carnegie Hall had been packed and why so many people had brought copies of *Trees* for the Man of the Trees. From then on I was known to Lowell's seventy million listeners as the Man of the Trees.

"You can't call yourself a forester till you have seen the California Coast redwoods," said Claudia Skipworth Coles, my first Bahá'í friend from the U.S.A.

I had long dreamt of these wonder trees and wished to be able to make a pilgrimage to see them. Members of the Society of American Foresters were urging me to visit them and give them a hand in preparing a constructive forest policy for their country. Sir Horace Plunkett, first Chairman of the Men of the Trees, had introduced me to Madison Grant, Founder of Save the Redwoods League, who had invited me to collaborate with him in his effort to save some groves of redwoods before it was too late. I worked my way across the country lecturing to philosophical societies and schools, interesting them in the work of the Men of the Trees in Palestine.

My first glimpse of the redwoods was at the Bohemian Grove where members of the Bohemian Club produce Grove Plays for their friends. Their stage is beautifully set with a back-drop of redwoods through which actors approach the stage along winding paths down the hillside. The audience sit on fallen tree-trunks. I was impressed by the beautiful setting and the idea of presenting plays especially written for the redwood groves, and went in search of a similar setting on a larger scale which could become a Grove of Understanding, and a place of pilgrimage for tree lovers and all Men of the Trees.

I had lectured to the Conservation Committee of the Garden Clubs of America and had interested them in forming a grove of their own. Save the Redwoods League had concentrated on saving individual trees or groves to be named in memory of individuals and families who had contributed to the purchase of these. My immediate concern was to save a large enough area to retain the local climate and I felt that at least twelve thousand acres would be required to be effective. From San Francisco I went northwards along the Redwood Empire Highway in search of the finest grove. Each district in California claimed that they had the tallest or biggest tree and each was anxious to have my help in preserving their tree. Tremendous inroads were being made into the virgin forest by great milling companies and often a forest fire would follow in the train of the lumberjacks.

As I proceeded north the groves of coast redwoods, towering to three hundred feet or more, became more beautiful; they were at their best with the sun lighting their trunks through the coast mists. Approaching Crescent City in Del Norte country I turned off to the right and followed a road which wound through the tall trees, their clean boles rising a hundred and fifty feet or more. Azaleas and rhododendrons with tree ferns formed the carpet of the forest floor. A clear spring rose at the feet of the tallest trees and flowed into Mill Creek. It was here that I came upon superb trees representing the supreme achievement of tree growth in the world today. Here it seemed that my search for the beautiful had ended. This, I decided, must be known as the Grove of Understanding. It was here that I visualized international plays and youth gatherings. What better setting could there be in which to plan the better world of tomorrow? I thought of Stanton A. Coblentz's lines on the redwoods which had been sent to me by one of our members:

> *I think that could the weary world but know*
> *Communion with these spirits breathing peace*
> *Strangely a veil would lift, a light would glow,*
> *And the dark tumult of our lives would cease.*

Among the trees I found circle upon circle and traced life back for nine thousand years. That night I camped in a hollow redwood tree which had been occupied for hundreds of years before me by Red Indians, for to the right of the entrance I dug up broken arrow-heads.

My journey took me on to British Columbia and on Vancouver Island I found the finest Douglas trees of all; they were growing in association with the Western Red Cedar beyond Cameron Lake and Campbell River. It was Dr. McLaren, the Park Superintendent of the Golden Gate, San Francisco, who told me the story of Douglas who had been sent out to California by the London Horticultural Society to collect seeds from the trees of the North-West Pacific. Once he was walking along the coast when he came across a huge cone that had been washed down one of the rivers and carried by the tide to the beach. He had seen nothing as large as this. On meeting an Indian he inquired in sign language where this came from. The Indian indicated by the angle of his chin a great distance up in the forest. Douglas searched the whole day and when night came he slept under the stars. At dawn he met another Indian and again in sign language inquired where he could find the tree from which this great cone came. This Indian indicated in the same direction, further on. It was not until the evening of the third day that Douglas was able to match the cone to the tree — the sugar pine, *pinus lambertiana*, greatest of all pines.

From there Douglas went on in search of new species, coming at last to the tree now named after him. There were clusters of cones high up in the branches and with his shot-gun he tried to shoot these down. So intent was he on his marksmanship that he did not notice that he had been silently surrounded by Indians, who firmly disarmed him as they thought the poor fellow had taken leave of his senses. It took some time to make them understand what he was after; when he succeeded they were only too willing to co-operate with him, with the result that he was able to ship a large consignment of seed back to London.

From California he went on to Honolulu, still searching for new species and here, unfortunately, he fell into a pit, a spiked buffalo trap, and was gored to death by its furious occupant. Two days later natives found his little dog, patiently waiting near the trap for his master's return.

It is fitting that one of the finest timber trees of the world should be named Douglas after one who gave his life for his love of trees.

These trees too were threatened by the lumberman's axe and I hoped that some virgin groves would be set aside so that future generations might enjoy them in their pristine glory. Excitedly I went from tree to tree photographing them, though the Ranger who was with me warned me that it was time to leave to catch my boat at Victoria. I insisted on his featuring in further studies before I consented to return with him. A few miles from the port we were held up by a lumber train on a level crossing, and although we drove furiously we arrived only in time to see the boat leaving the harbour.

"I shall catch it at San Francisco," I said, and thanked my Ranger friend, who passed me on to other foresters. They drove me by stages along the Redwood Empire Highway back to San Francisco. I have always been glad that I missed the boat at Victoria, for it gave me an opportunity of viewing the Coast Redwoods from a different direction. By the time I reached San Francisco I was convinced that my first choice—the Mill Creek woods with the Grove of Understanding—had been right.

I caught the boat and went on my way to Tahiti and Rarotonga, working my way to New Zealand, splicing steel cable before the mast and lending the ship's carpenter a hand. A huge basket of fresh fruit had been sent to me on board by one of Claudia's Baha'i friends and this lasted me until I was able to take on fresh supplies at Rarotonga.

At Wellington I was met by Sir Francis Dillon Bell, the first Minister of Forests, who took advantage of my visit to step up the State planting programme, providing work for farmers who were then getting only threepence a pound for their wool. Planting at Kaingaroa was brought up to 22,000 acres a year. I prepared a plan for the New Zealand Perpetual Forests which also resulted in the planting of 22,000 acres a year.

I kept in touch with Lowell Thomas and wrote to him of an amusing experience on the Franz Joseph glacier. I was lying on the ice waiting for the sun to come out so that I could film the tree ferns growing near the edge of the glacier. After some minutes the sun obliged and I got an excellent shot. When I tried to get up, however, I found that my tweed jacket had frozen solidly into the glacier. Fortunately I was rescued by a friendly Maori, otherwise I might have been slowly carried down towards the sea. After that experience I went up to Rotorua to thaw out in the hot pools!

In Australia I prepared forestry planting plans for two more afforestation companies before visiting Mildura to bring the orange groves into my film, *The Romance of the Orange*. I wanted to influence people in England to eat two more oranges per head per year: Australian oranges. I knew that this would make all the difference between failure and success for the returned servicemen who had invested in orange groves. Sir Harold Clapp arranged for me to take half a shipload of oranges back with me to try them on the Liverpool and Manchester markets.

While filming the sea in the Bight, a huge wave washed me down the companion way, crushing my leg against the iron railing. The wound became infected and I was put ashore at Colombo. By the time a Tamil surgeon arrived tetanic poisoning had set in. He wanted to amputate the leg or, he said, the poison would go to my heart, which would be fatal. I was unable to speak but wrote on a piece of paper:

"I am a forester. I need both legs."

He agreed to postpone the operation till the next day, when I put him off again. He gave me up in disgust and went on his way. My Singalese boy made poultices from the leaves of a native tree, but in spite of his efforts I seemed to get worse. Sure that my end had come, I wrote my last Will and Testament in the form of a letter to Claudia. In it I sent messages to the Men of the Trees and described the Mill Creek groves of redwoods with the Grove of Understanding which had meant so much to me. I begged her to save the grove. My letter was posted. I lost consciousness, and during the next three days my spirit seemed to drift back to the redwoods and bask in the glorious shafts of sunshine streaming through the groves of earth's oldest living trees. But slowly life returned. I regained consciousness and three weeks later I was able to get up and broadcast in three languages.

When I got to Mt. Carmel I learned that Claudia had died the day before I had written to her. In London I called on her daughter, who handed me the letter I had written from Ceylon. I had been spared to fulfil the mission which in extremity I had entrusted to another.

On my return to England after my first world tour, the salvation of the Californian Coast redwoods became the most important thing in my life. I was introduced to Mr. Tillemont Thompson of the Lecture Agency by my friend Gilbert. My first booking was at Picton Hall, Liverpool, which Thompson regarded as a test audience for his lecturers. My subject was "Adventures of a Forester in Kenya and in the Mahogany Forests in Nigeria", illustrated with slides I had taken myself. Luckily for me, the lecture was a success.

With the co-operation of the Lecture Agency I arranged to present my new lecture on "Wonder Trees of the World" on a nation-wide basis. While still sending part of the proceeds of my lectures to the Men of the Trees in Palestine, I launched a Save the Redwoods Fund under the patronage of Sir Francis Younghusband, who had become the first President of the Men of the Trees in Britain. Starting in Manchester I lectured throughout the country on the redwoods and met with a very generous response to my appeals for help. After this tour I sailed for New York on the first stage of my mission.

As my boat approached New York journalists came aboard. As usual the first question was, "What do you think of America?"— a question I feel I still cannot answer adequately, even after fourteen visits there. The next question was, "What do you think of the war debts?" At this time, of course, the subject was widely discussed. "War debts!" I exclaimed. "I'm far too busy thinking of much more important things. Do you know that last year you destroyed by fire in your forests twice as much as we paid you in gold the other day?"

That evening I went on the air with Lowell Thomas in *World News*. He introduced me in his usual lively fashion: "Hello everybody! Who do you think is with me on the air tonight? The Man of the Trees. He's been planting trees in Palestine, he's visited the groves of the oldest living trees, in California, he's seen the kauris in New Zealand, the giant eucalyptus trees in Australia, he's met the tree worshippers in Ceylon and no doubt worshipped with them, and now here he is, back again, just as much in love with trees as ever. I believe he'll marry a tree one of these days! Where are you off to this time, Man of the Trees?"

"I'm off to California, to the redwoods—the wonder trees of the world. Tree lovers in England have given their money to help save these groves, and now I'm on my way to the redwoods to form a Grove of Understanding, a Mecca for tree lovers from all over the world. These trees are your heritage from the past—what are you doing for the future?"

At the end of the broadcast, a multi-millionaire rang up and said, "Mr. Thomas, I want to talk to the Man of the Trees who was on your programme tonight. Would you bring him round to lunch tomorrow?"

When I met him, his first question was, "Do you mean to say that over-taxed Englishmen are sending out their dimes and their quarters to save our redwood trees?"

"Yes, sir," I replied.

"Why?"

"Because they love them."

"But how can they love them if they haven't seen them?"

"They've seen my pictures. And on the eve of my departure I gave an illustrated lecture at the Royal Geographical Society in London before a very representative audience. They feel that Americans have done so much in the past in the cause of science and humanity for the world through England, that it is time that England did something for the world through America, and the best thing they can do is to help you save your glorious redwoods. You've been up there, you've seen them, haven't you?"

He shook his head.

"But," I said, "do you mean to say that you, an American multi-millionaire, have never seen these trees for yourself? You must remedy this straightaway. Please let me use your telephone to get on to the Secretary of Save the Redwoods League."

When I met him again on his return from seeing the redwoods, he gave half a million dollars—the first substantial gift. Later Rockefeller made a gift of three and a half million dollars, which went into saving the redwoods at Bull Creek flats. But the great majority of subscriptions were small donations, starting at ten cents.

The urgency for action was emphasized by Sheriff Breen and Fred Endert of Crescent City, who informed me that the groves I had chosen were threatened because eighteen million feet of their timber was needed for boards to pour cement into in the construction of the new Golden Gate bridge at San Francisco. One Thursday we busied ourselves ringing up the Press of California, for we had arranged a meeting in the groves on the Sunday afternoon and we wanted to have a representative gathering. The Press were most helpful, with the result that people from far and near joined us in the Grove of Understanding. I told them how much their trees meant to me and how I felt that in years to come these trees would make the same strong appeal to thousands who would visit them from all over the world; that these trees, now threatened for their timber, would be far more valuable if protected now; and that the Men of the Trees in England had sent their gifts as a 'thank you' to America. I appealed to the lumbermen to stay their hand and give me an opportunity to raise the money required to buy the trees back on the timber cruisers' valuation. Three days later they met together, responded generously to my appeal and obtained the lumber for the Golden Gate bridge from other sources.

It took me nine years to create sufficient interest and raise enough funds, but those lumbermen were true to their promise. When it came to acquiring the trees they accepted only a proportion of what they were worth. I was impressed that these hardheaded businessmen had shared my vision.

From then on for the next eight years I would arrive in California about the first day of spring and drive north from San Diego, lecturing and broadcasting and gaining the support of an ever-widening public. However, by 1939 my Mill Creek Grove was still a project, and much of the money that I had been raising was being spent saving other groves farther south, such as the Bull Creek flats which absorbed seven and a half million dollars. It was then that I decided it was necessary to form a deputation of Men of the Trees from England to support me in my fight to save the Mill Creek Groves. After a nation-wide tour and the planting of trees to commemorate the Royal Visit, we arrived at Crescent City and were taken by our members there to explore the boundaries of the groves we were trying to save. Everyone shared my view about the value of these trees. Once again the Press came to our help and our project was given publicity. The first nine thousand acres were taken over by the State of California and we persuaded the Forestry Department to contribute a further three thousand acres as a natural reserve. So my target of twelve thousand acres was achieved and handed over to the State of California to be preserved for all time.

In his acceptance speech, Mr. Gleeson, speaking for California, said, "In setting aside these groves of redwoods we're doing not

KIAMA REUNION 1953

Chief Joseph Nionjo welcoming the Baba Wa Muthi, Father of the Tree, during the emergency, after an absence of thirty years.

REUNION IN KIKUYULAND

The author is welcomed back to Kikuyuland by his old friend Thotho Thongo who was head Moran at the first dance of the trees. This event, on July 22, 1922, resulted in the planting of millions of trees in Kenya and the founding of a world movement with the co-operation of 108 countries.

ST. BARBE AND 'THE GHOST'.

During the Cobbetts Rural Ride, St. Barbe and 'The Ghost' covered 330 miles in 20 days giving talks on trees to 73 schools.

MT. COOK STATION

Located in the New Zealand high country, Mt. Cook Station serves as an overseas headquarters of Men of the Trees and the Sahara Reclamation Project.

only a wonderful thing for California and the nation but for the whole world, for these trees are unequalled in beauty and age. They are among the oldest living trees on earth and if protected now will endure through the millennia."

Patriotic Women's Clubs of America created interest to save a further five thousand acres near by as a National Tribute Grove to the Fallen, bringing the total area up to seventeen thousand acres. A permanent camp was established with an arena for camp-fire gatherings. In 1960 the Men of the Trees marked the twenty-first anniversary of saving the first twelve thousand acres by holding a reunion in the Grove of Understanding.

Chapter 6

THE BALLOON HAS GONE UP!

My strength is as the strength of ten,
Because my heart is pure.
Sir Galahad. ALFRED LORD TENNYSON

I N 1938 I met the editor and founder of *The Countryman*, Robertson Scott, at Idbury, Kingham, in Oxfordshire. He invited me to come over to tea—I had long wanted to meet one who had made such a tremendous contribution to country ways and country life.

As I entered his office he rose and welcomed me with genuine affection as if we had been lifelong friends. He came straight to the point. "I want you to write something for *The Countryman*. Here is your title: 'The Way by Which I Have Come'. This will be the first in a new series of articles by men and women who have made a contribution towards rural life. I want you to describe in a simple way your awakening to a need for the countryside, what you have tried to do, your successes and your failures and the lessons you have learnt." The article appeared in *The Countryman* in July 1938.

The first Summer School of the Men of the Trees was convened at Oxford in the same year. Oxford was chosen because the Imperial Forestry Institute was there with its lecturers on various branches of forestry. Accommodation was provided at Lady Margaret Hall and one hundred and fifty members were in residence for ten days. There were four papers read each week-day morning and expeditions were arranged to surrounding wooded estates each afternoon; there was an illustrated lecture each evening, including one public lecture.

One of the papers, prepared by the Director, Mr. Austin, and read by the First Secretary of the American Embassy in London, released news of the Tree Genetic Station at Placerville, California. Members were particularly interested in this Institute, founded by

Mr. Eddy, a lumber-king, whom I had had the pleasure of meeting at the London home of Mrs. Graham Murray.

He had come to my club to discuss what could be done for the future of trees and forestry. He had explained that his wealth had been built up from what the forest yielded and that he would like to devote a proportion of this to research in a branch of forestry which would make the greatest contribution to future timber supplies. I had been impressed by the pioneer tree-breeding technique of Luther Burbank, particularly his walnut experiments, but so far nothing had been done towards the breeding of soft woods. I therefore suggested to Mr. Eddy that there was a wide field open in the cross-pollination of pines with the object of improving form and growth. He readily accepted this suggestion and on his return to California purchased a favourable site and started a large-scale experiment in the cross-pollination of selected species of pine native to California. On the face of it, this would seem to be a long-term investment, for one would hardly expect cones to be produced under ten or fifteen years; but in the course of cross-pollinating some of the progeny showed precocity, cones being produced much earlier than expected. This led to the cross-pollination of precocious species, with the result that not only was superior timber produced but the time for seed-bearing was reduced to a minimum. Each year I visited these experiments at Placerville and encouraged the Director, so it was appropriate that I should include a paper on the Tree Genetic Station at the first Summer School.

Another paper concerned Professor Douglas's work in Tucson, Arizona. Here he carried out his fascinating experiments on tree rings and chronology. He had discovered that there was a series of broad rings, followed by narrower rings; the broader rings, he found, coincided with sunspots. The Professor, an astronomer and a mathematician, was able to observe a definite cycle of broad and narrow rings, and, working on material obtained from wooden remains in ancient cities and Indian villages, he was able to construct a composite core dating back for about two thousand years. When, in the course of excavations, an archæologist wanted to date the town or village, he would make borings of the material and take these to the key core and be able to date his find. This

new science of tree rings and chronology, which I named dendrochronology, was not only useful to the archæologist but to the
farmer and the forester; rainfall was found to recur in very definite
cycles and could thus be predicted. Knowledge of these recurring
cycles was also of value in meteorology. For the first time the
science of dendrochronology was brought to Europe and the
paper prepared by Professor Douglas was read out.

Cambridge was chosen unaimously for the next Summer
School.

Plans went ahead for the 1939 Summer School to be held in
Newham College and Margaret Tennant became Summer School
Secretary.

In the spring of 1939 I had agreed to conduct a party of the
Men of the Trees to the U.S.A. on a nation-wide tour following
the Royal Visit of our King and Queen. It was arranged in con-
junction with the English Speaking Union, and at the time of my
departure to New York to lecture at the World Fair as many as
thirty-six members had sent in their names, desiring to be in the
party. But as the days went by the majority were deterred by the
threat of war. Finally only six sailed in the new *Berengaria* with
Lilian Messer, the Honorary Treasurer, while I was working
desperately hard to make a success of the tour, arranging for
planting ceremonies in New York, Washington, Los Angeles and
other places to mark the Royal Visit.

Before leaving the United Kingdom I was concerned that I
should entrust the editing of our journal *Trees* to competent
hands and we were fortunate in being able to persuade Diana
Buist to take this responsibility. She had come with her father,
Colonel Frederick Buist, to the first Summer School at Oxford in
1938 and I had been impressed by her depth of character and
wisdom. She was reserved, yet had a remarkable capacity for
friendship. She was greatly admired, especially by our younger
members, and proved to be a tower of strength to Marjory Mumm,
the Honorary Secretary, who was almost overwhelmed at times by
the amount of correspondence that flooded the office. Miss
Kershaw and Miss Foster, who dealt with the Forestry Association
of Great Britain, as well as my mail and the Society's mail, were
always grateful for her advice and assistance in tackling current

problems that had to be dealt with at our Studio Headquarters at 2 Jays Mews, Kensington, which was soon to be evacuated for our wartime Country Headquarters at Manor Farm, Puncknowle in Dorset. Marjory had been horrified at the thought of leaving London where all her life she had been dependent on her mother and old family servants. It was Diana's reassuring and confident outlook that encouraged her to take the plunge and supervise the staff at our Puncknowle Headquarters for the next six years, during which time she endeared herself to many of the members she met and with whom she corresponded during the war years.

But I am going too fast. Although war clouds were gathering over Europe the general belief was that England could not possibly be involved, as we were quite unprepared for war, and so plans for the next Summer School at Cambridge went ahead. During my nation-wide tour with Lilla Messer and six outstanding members, Headquarters became busier than ever and much of my work in connection with the Forestry Commission, the Forestry Association of Great Britain, as well as the Men of the Trees, fell to Diana. The responsibility of a temporary editor is always considerable. There is the date-line for the printer, proofs to be corrected, contributors to be encouraged and some would-be contributors to be kept at bay. There is always a spate of amateur poetic effusions. Diana handled every situation with ability and tact, only allowing the best to go to press.

The responsibility of arranging accommodation for the 1939 Summer School devolved on Margaret Tennant. Numbers were limited to one hundred and fifty members and the College Bursar insisted that this be an exact figure. Experience had proved that there were always the unavoidable last-minute cancellations which had to be filled from a waiting list. In those days summer schools were in their infancy and this was only our second. It must have been a harassing experience for poor Margaret, so many were the likes and dislikes of the members. One 'scientific' member insisted that he must sleep with his feet towards the magnetic north! Picture the painstaking Summer School Secretary with a pocket compass exploring room after room to discover a bed in which that member would be properly orientated! Another member who had booked for himself and his wife wrote a lengthy letter saying that as a rule he and his wife took their holidays separately. He went on to explain to the long-suffering secretary that as they were both tree-lovers they did not want to miss the Summer School, but that they insisted on separate bedrooms.

Nineteen-thirty-nine was a memorable year for the Men of the Trees. As a result of an address I gave the members of the House of Commons and members of the 1922 Committee, I was informed by Lord Altrincham that the King wished me to go to the Palace to see if arrangements could be made for him to visit the Civilian Conservation Corps at Fort Hunt, near Washington. It took about six months' negotiation between Buckingham Palace and the White House to bring this about. After their visit to Canada, the Royal Party came to Washington, inspected the dockyards and visited Fort Hunt.

For some time I had been wanting to establish something like the Civilian Conservation Corps in Great Britain; I was hoping that if the King, who was interested in boys' camps, commented favourably, this would encourage the British Government to launch a similar progressive movement for youth.

On the day of the Royal visit I invited my old friend, Bill Lancaster Jenkins, of Gwyned, Pennsylvania, to lunch with me at the Cosmos Club in Washington. (He was the only other non-African present when I started the *Watu wa Miti* in the highlands of Kenya in 1922.) He offered to drive me to Fort Hunt and we reached it about four minutes before the Royal Party arrived.

While President Roosevelt remained in his car, Robert Fechner, Director of the C.C.C., conducted the King and Queen through the camp. One lad, who came from Scotland, was presented to the Queen. "Why did you leave our beautiful country to come out here?" she asked. The lad replied, "For work and opportunity, Ma'am. I didn't get run out!" She still seemed surprised that anyone should want to leave her beloved Scotland. However, as always, she endeared herself to everyone.

The visit of some of the Men of the Trees to the United States which I organized and led in 1939 went off well, even though the numbers were small. Each day seemed more wonderful than the previous one. We covered about 18,000 miles, not only generating goodwill between the two countries, but also helping to clinch the final saving of the first 12,000 acres of redwoods at Mill Creek near Crescent City.

We returned in time for the Cambridge Summer School and thanks to Margaret Tennant an attractive programme was awaiting the one hundred and fifty members who came into residence at Newnham College for a memorable ten days of lectures and expeditions. Many members have said that but for the inspiration of that Summer School on the eve of the outbreak of war they could never have borne the terrifying experiences of the Battle of Britain. Personally, I recall with gratitude the help given by Major Patrick Synge, Major-General Walter Hill and Lord Wedgwood, who, each in turn, presided at my lectures. My old friends, Messrs. Rolls-Royce, generously lent me their latest model to pick up our President, Colonel Sir Francis Younghusband, and drive him to Cambridge for the opening day. It was a strange coincidence that just on the eve of the outbreak of World War II I should find myself only a few yards from the college where I had been at the outbreak of World War I.

The night that war was declared, I was on duty at the House of Commons, standing by with other members of the Metropolitan Mounted Branch. At three o'clock the next morning I took my horse back to the stables and went to my room and found a naval officer there. He had bought my old Hillman 6/16 but was now returning it, as I had promised to buy it back from him at the end of his leave. I decided to drive him back to Portsmouth. On my way to Putney I called at Walham Green, my wartime mounted police depot, to report for duty. I asked the Inspector if he would be good enough to have my horse led to Kempton Park and promised to make up for my absence that day, by going on night duty. He kindly consented to arrange this, and we drove on our way. As we reached Kingston the first siren of the war sounded. In seconds all the people on the pavements seemed to disappear underground. As we sped through Esher we were directed off the main road and told to park, but we kept going until we reached a cordon of special constabulary who allowed us to proceed at our own discretion. We kept going and eventually worked our way round to the main road a few miles further on. This time there was a very businesslike-looking cordon across the road. I put on my steel helmet, stepped on the accelerator and was allowed to pass!

The roads were empty and we cruised at our usual 95 m.p.h. in the old Hillman. Approaching Churt, I remembered that I was due to lunch with friends that very Sunday, so I drove up to the house. The butler opened the door and informed us there had been a raid on London.

"Where did you get that news from?" I asked. He said the chauffeur's daughter had rung up and told them and had asked that her father be allowed to come up and rescue her. He had already gone. The butler assured me there had been a "terrible raid" and that bombs were dropping right and left.

"How dare you talk like that!" I exclaimed. "It's a beautiful morning and there's not an enemy plane in sight. I've just come from London."

My friends were delighted to welcome me and at one o'clock the news came through that an unidentified plane had been sighted off Dover; this had prompted the siren which had caused all the panic.

Leaving the young officer at Whale Island to report for duty I drove back to Woking where my new caravan trailer was being fitted with black-out curtains by Lilian Messer. I took it in tow and drove to Kempton Park race-course where I reported for night duty.

The mounted branch took on the patrolling of London water supply and released a large number of foot police who were reservists for service overseas. There were days when we enjoyed troop drill, reminding me of King Edward's Horse in the early days of World War I. We could not have wished for a better crowd of people and I enjoyed the comradeship of men who had served in many campaigns.

One day a very handsome roman-nosed chestnut arrived. It was a gift from Lord Lonsdale. It had killed a groom by crushing him against the wall of its stable but the creature was so handsome his owner was loath to shoot it. Having a high opinion of the mounted branch's unequalled experience with horses, he felt sure they would be able to tame even this outlaw. I was passing the Inspector when the horse arrived. "Baker," he said, "you're the oldest man here. You'd better ride that brute."

I enjoyed riding him but after ten days of good behaviour, while I was saddling him, he suddenly crushed me against the wall, splintering three ribs. I drove myself to the doctor and was put into plaster. Then I returned to complete saddling the horse and did a patrol of eighteen miles, bringing him back to his stall without mishap. However, I got some sick leave to enable me to go back to my timber production work which I had undertaken for the Ministry of Supply. My district stretched from East Sussex up to and including the Duchy of Cornwall.

While at Oxford, marking timber at Wytham Abbey, I had a telephone call from Major-General Walter Hill, who asked me if I would take care of a little coloured boy who had escaped from the torpedoed *Simon Bolivar* and was waiting at the West African Students' Club in London. I caught the next train to Paddington and from there went by bus. Just outside St. Martin-in-the-Fields, Howard Coster, the photographer, jumped on my bus with the words: "I knew you were in London, St. Barbe. I've been ringing your club and they told me you weren't here."

He was excited that we had met in this extraordinary way. He quickly explained why he particularly wanted to see me. He wanted me to speak to Sir Alan Lascelles, the King's private secretary, on behalf of thousands of people like himself who were occupied with their business during the day but would be prepared to go on guard at night. This was at the height of the Battle of Britain and the reverse at Dunkirk had aroused the nation to a pitch of patriotic fervour unknown before.

We got off the bus at Bedford Square. I telephoned Sir Alan who listened and explained that the Queen of Holland had just arrived and the King was far too busy, so he would get Anthony Eden to broadcast this to the nation. Howard Coster's idea was that if the King himself made an appeal, a million people would volunteer the next day. As it happened, half-a-million did volunteer within twenty-four hours.

When I got back to Puncknowle, my wartime headquarters, with my little coloured friend from the *Simon Bolivar* I was in time to hear Eden's moving broadcast to the nation, and with the lads of the village I joined the Local Defence Volunteers, as the Home Guard was first called.

My particular job came under the auspices of the War Office and as I was constantly receiving secret documents indicating the latest measurements of poles to be erected as obstructions to enemy aeroplanes attempting to land in the South of England, my district coinciding with the area in which I was supervising timber supplies, I christened myself "Chief Obstructionist"!

I shall always remember the excitement of the day that Clayton Davis, Honorary Secretary of the *Tree Lovers' Calendar*, asked me to collect the *Calendar* files from his flat in Kensington. A stick of bombs had been dropped across the square and the area was cordoned off. Only one of the five bombs had exploded.

There was no one around when I arrived in my car, so I moved the barrier far enough to let my car through and drove up to Clayton's house. On entering the basement I found an Irish maid crouching beneath the kitchen table, waiting for the next explosion. I asked her if she was all right and had enough food, seized the *Calendar* files and bolted back in triumph to my car.

When I presented Clayton with the files, however, he exclaimed, "But you've left out the drawer of the S's—and it has the largest number of subscribers!"

Early the next morning I ran the gauntlet again. Two more bombs had exploded in the meantime, and the last remaining inhabitant of the square, the Irish maid, was still hiding under the kitchen table! When I had found the drawer of the S's I tried to persuade the girl to leave the house and come with me to safety. She remained adamant, convinced that she would be safer in the house than anywhere else.

I and the missing drawer of the file escaped unscathed; but I often wonder what happened to my lone Irish maid.

Before the outbreak of the war, I had started a Forestry Training Centre at Greenleaze, Puncknowle in Dorset. The training combined theory and practice, starting with twenty minutes' intensive theory each morning, followed by work in the woods or nurseries for the rest of the day. We lived simply in our reed-thatched cottage. "What shall we have for lunch?" we would say, then go out into the garden and get it. In the mackerel fishing season my forestry students might go down to the shore to help haul in a catch and be invited to take all they needed. Milk and bread were provided by

Puncknowle Manor and delivered by the keeper in the course of his daily rounds. If by any chance I was called away in connection with my Ministry of Supply or silvicultural work, my students would carry on as if I were present, keeping a record of the number of man-hours devoted to each operation and electing one of the group to be responsible for the forestry lesson each morning.

Returning from one of my expeditions, I was met by the old keeper and upon inquiring how things were going, he seemed satisfied that all was well and told me that the previous evening he had found my students working on the Knowle weeding a young plantation. That was after seven in the evening and upon inquiring why they were working so late, they explained to him that they had had to take shelter in a downpour at noon and were making up for lost time. These were the men who became leaders in forestry and set the pace for generations of forestry students at home and overseas.

Throughout the war, while marking timber for the Ministry of Supply to keep local mills working to capacity and to satisfy timber importers, I insisted that for every tree felled at least one should be planted. To this end the honorary treasurer of the Men of the Trees launched the *Million Shilling Planting Fund* to assist landowners to re-stock denuded areas. This fund was not only the means of replenishing trees in many parts of England that had been sacrificed to war needs, but it attracted many new members to the Men of the Trees, amongst them Bernard Shaw.

I had met him between the wars at a party for authors and we had got on to the subject of trees. Shaw said, "I'm only interested in cutting them down." So I wrote to him at the time of the launching of our planting fund, suggesting that the war was probably cutting them down fast enough to please even him! I said I thought it would do him no harm, and me a lot of good, if he wrote a few words in our favour and became a member of our Society!

He replied by return.

"Upon the little summer house where I write my plays, thousands of acorns shower themselves down. For the past thirty years I've collected many of these and gone round the lanes and byways and, like Nelson's Admiral Collingwood, I've dibbled them in with my stick but they will not grow for me. During the past five years

I have been sending the acorns to Lord So-and-so's forester and now you may see row upon row of oak saplings raised from the acorns of my collecting, but they will not grow for me. Is my hand accursed? You're doing a fine job of work and I'm entirely in sympathy with your aims. I shall be happy if you will accept me as a Life Fellow. I'm an old man so I shall not burden your Society very long. I enclose my cheque."

I replied,

" Dear Mr. Shaw,
     My Council will be delighted to accept you as a Life Fellow of the Men of the Trees. Now that you have become one of us the curse, if any, will be removed and all your little acorns will grow for you.
     We wish you:
          ' The health of the pines
          The strength of an oak
          And the endurance of a Redwood tree.' "

Shaw invited me to come and see him whenever I was in his part of the country. In gratitude for his generous support I presented him with a copy of *Among the Trees* with a picture of a giant sequoia I had taken in Sequoia National Park during the Men of the Trees' expedition. It was taken at noon when the sun was directly overhead. When I printed the picture there were the twin heads of Bernard Shaw with his high forehead and bearded face, deep-set eyes as if he had been immortalized in the indestructible bark of one of the oldest living trees on earth. Later, when he became ill, Shaw kept the book by his bedside and was proud to show it to visitors.

The toll of the war on our timber supplies was heavy, but wherever I went I found the landowners enthusiastic to give their full quota to the war effort. King George himself particularly wished to set a good example to landowners on his woodlands in the Duchy of Cornwall, which came under my technical supervision. In fact he insisted on sacrificing far more than the scientific management of his estates could afford. I was particularly anxious that the Duchy woodlands should not suffer too severely from this over-cutting and proposed to my Council of the Men of the Trees that a grant of trees from the Million Shilling Planting Fund should be made available to the Royal plantations. These young trees were gratefully received by the Secretary to the Duchy and were planted under my personal supervision and that of the Steward.

My experience in life and work in any good cause has been that it is impossible to please everybody, and my action in recommending the Duchy for this grant was strongly criticized by some members of the Men of the Trees' Council and others, who objected on the grounds that the King was able to buy his own trees. My contention was that the King had made greater sacrifices than any landowners known to me and that his need was therefore greater. Besides this, I was confident that the little trees would be well cared for in the Duchy plantations. Eventually the dissenters came to accept my point of view.

As far as possible I saw to it that all the fellings were in the nature of improvement fellings and throughout the many estates under my supervision in the South of England I had ruled out clear felling as impracticable and uneconomic. I felt that it was essential to retain tree-cover, especially on hillsides, and not allow the tree beauty to be sacrificed as a panic measure. Looking back on the war years perhaps my greatest contribution was the saving of these woodlands from complete destruction by Military Forestry Corps from New Zealand, Australia and Canada. I was not successful in Scotland, where the Canadian Forestry Corps had fifty-four camps and cleared whole hillsides, resulting in disastrous erosion and untold damage to the country's economy.

As it was impossible to protect our office at 2 Jays Mews in Kensington, I had taken the Manor Farm, Puncknowle, for six years or so. Mrs. Palmer, lady of the Manor, had generously waived rent for the first year and had undertaken to put in a bathroom and carry out other necessary improvements. I built a lean-to greenhouse into which I made a door from the office and full use was made of the garden, which had been rested for at least a dozen years. I constructed a large compost heap from old railway sleepers and very soon was returning to the land more than was being taken out of it. Clayton Davis, Calendar Secretary, came to assist us in the work. Although physically handicapped he was mentally very alert and we all greatly appreciated his courage and advice. He had previously held a very responsible position in the motor world. It was a happy team that occupied the war-time headquarters of the Men of the Trees in the little village of Puncknowle, and soon we were accepted by the villagers as part of their community.

To enable us to live and work more intimately with the villagers I rented an allotment from the Manor property, for seven and sixpence a year. In this we were able to grow extra food such as potatoes, silver-beet, cabbages, etc. Sometimes we would have advanced students of forestry and agriculture amongst our volunteers, who were taking a working holiday to help us at headquarters. They too would take their turn in the allotment, enjoying the hints given by the local allotment holders. One day a few thousand little pine trees arrived to be grown and, being short of room in my nurseries, I lined them out in my allotment, somewhat to the displeasure of the locals who explained that the allotments were to grow food, not trees.

"What are those trees doing there?" queried one of the older villagers.

"Those are my tea trees," I replied.

"What do you mean, tea trees?" he said.

I explained that owing to the shortage of shipping we were having to choose between importing timber and tea. My idea was that if we could grow more timber in Britain we could release a ship or two to bring in tea. They saw the point of taking a long-term view.

At Christmas time I would throw a party for the Commander and members of the Local Volunteers and there would be much cursing when their wellington boots were dragged off by the suction in the clay soil surrounding Greenleaze. However, these parties were a success and full justice was done to the refreshments provided, most members taking their turn to entertain the party with songs and recitations in typical Dorset style.

For the greater part, the Puncknowle forest was free from war alarms though the occasional German parachutist would be spotted by members of the Home Guard. However, all Puncknowle used to enjoy the air battles which occasionally enlivened the skies. The wardens would blow their whistles to no avail as the villagers ran up the hill to get the best view of the fight. One Saturday afternoon when three marauding planes were driven into the airspace above our headquarters the whole village crowded into our garden to get a grandstand view! It was an exciting battle which ended with all three planes being brought down in adjoining fields.

When the war was over and timber was no longer so urgently needed for the war effort and the heavy demands of the Normandy landings and the Forces had been met, I was able to relax with my forestry students at Greenleaze and make plans for training returning servicemen. I drew up a project on the lines of the Civilian Conservation Corps camps in America—the same plan as I had presented to Mr. Roosevelt while he was still Governor of New York.

The plan I made for Britain was called "The Landsmen". We had seamen and airmen, so why not landsmen? It was submitted to the Government and adopted in a modified form, though the title for the project was not officially used. Young farmers were becoming interested in forestry and my lectures were much in demand.

Chapter 7

LAUNCHING THE GREEN FRONT

I do not count the hours I spend
In wandering by the sea
The forest is my loyal friend
Like God it useth me.

Waldeinsamkeit. EMERSON

D URING THE WAR, Lord Mamhead succeeded Colonel Sir Francis Younghusband as President of the Men of the Trees. Our annual meetings were held at this time in the Hall of Puncknowle Manor; the *Journal* and the *Tree Lovers' Calendar* continued to be published, although in modified forms. Our exhibitions of tree pictures were held in Dorchester and Bath and lectures on trees and forestry were frequently given to philosophical societies and schools throughout the country. Parliament made headway in inaugurating a progressive forest policy and for the first time the Forestry Commission was enabled to establish official training centres for foresters and woodmen, apart from their old Forest of Dean School. The Million Shilling Planting Fund continued to fulfil the purpose for which it was launched and the greater percentage of the areas felled were replanted or regenerated within a few months of the end of the war, at any rate in the South of England.

While lecturing in Worcester I met Doreen Long, who had become my secretary and joined my two colleagues at Puncknowle. On January 23, 1946, we were married in the church of St. Mary's, Puncknowle, by my old friend, Bill Anderson, then Bishop of Portsmouth. As we left the church we passed under an arch of spades and axes—the novel idea of the local Home Guard who turned up in full force and afterwards joined the Bishop in the local inn to celebrate. The wedding breakfast was generously provided by Mrs. Palmer, in the beautiful oak-panelled Manor Hall.

Marjory Mumm, Clayton Davis and one of my old forestry pupils, John Finlayson, and the two other secretaries, held the fort at headquarters while Doreen and I enjoyed a honeymoon in Jersey. After a glorious three weeks of reunions with Jersey members who had brought their trees unscathed through the war, we returned to Puncknowle to work on my current book, *Green Glory, Forests of the World.* I was able to produce it with the co-operation of members of the Diplomatic Corps from forty-four countries who accepted my invitation to lunch at the Dorchester, Park Lane, and agreed to complete a forestry questionnaire. The book was published in the U.S.A. and in Germany, as well as in Britain. It was the German edition that won me an Honorary Life Fellowship of the Institute of Arts and Letters. Since then the book has become a textbook in the U.S.S.R., prompting the Russians to treble the Roosevelt shelter belt planting programme and achieve it in the same time.

As I was completing the last chapter, Angela, our first child, was born on November 4, 1946. Later we moved to the Gate Farm, Abbotsbury, where our son Paul was born on November 7, 1949.

While at the Gate I launched Tree Services for the care and repair of ornamental trees. I acquired two Red Cross vans to accommodate the two teams of three lads I trained. One stretcher was taken out of each van to allow room for the equipment necessary for climbing the tallest trees. One of the sights of London, in those days, was to see our teams working on branches near the top of the great plane trees. Their training included an appreciation of the artistic anatomy of trees and the art of lightening the heads of trees without lopping them. There were members in our teams who could walk up trees as easily as I could walk upstairs and their exploits attracted crowds of London sightseers. Many valuable trees that had been threatened were saved in this way and are still enjoyed by Londoners. The same was true in other cities, including Bath where the great planes of the Circle were saved by the Men of the Trees and our Tree Services.

I was also instrumental in bringing the Forestry Association of Great Britain into being at an inaugural luncheon at the Dorchester, presided over by the Earl of Portsmouth who had written the forward to my book, *I Planted Trees.* This book had been dictated to two secretaries in ten days while I had influenza. It was the means of recruiting many young men and leading them to devote their lives to work in forestry. Some years later I was complaining to my publisher that I had never succeeded in writing a best-seller. He thought for a minute and then replied, "I wouldn't say that, because we sold thirty-two thousand copies of *I Planted Trees.*"

This successful book was followed by *Africa Drums*, published in the first instance by Lindsay Drummond and later by George Ronald, and by Wellington Books in the U.S.A. It also went into many editions and was published in French and Norwegian. I was very grateful for the royalties from Norway, which were to be of great help to me in the future.

I arranged the first Summer School after the war, at my old school Dean Close, Cheltenham, with the help of the Headmaster, who afterwards became Headmaster of St. Paul's, London. This Summer School included expeditions to surrounding wooded estates in Gloucestershire, including the Forest of Dean and Lidney, the seat of Lord Bledisloe, who had been a popular Governor-General of New Zealand and for forty-seven years Honorary Verderer of the Forest of Dean. Later he became President of the Men of the Trees, succeeding Lord Courthope of Whiligh in Sussex. At this historic Summer School, Sir Shane Leslie cabled the President of Ireland, suggesting he invite us to Eire the following year. By return cable he received an enthusiastic welcome.

Nineteen-forty-seven marked the climax of Men of the Trees' Schools Branch, started by Evelyn Harbord from Powdermill House, Battle Abbey. Many lectures were given to the schools and forestry made steady progress both under the Forestry Commission and on estates that had come under the Dedication Scheme.

Our visit to Ireland the following year will always be remembered by the huge gathering at Phœnix Park, when the President entertained the Men of the Trees not only from England but from Northern Ireland and Eire. Seven hundred and fifty guests were welcomed to a wonderful strawberry tea-party after a ceremonial planting of nine Atlas cedars in the Park. The senior Cardinal officiated, assisted by acolytes carrying holy water and the whole procedure was most impressive. During the tea-party I asked the President what percentage of Eire was tree-covered and ventured to suggest that it might be two-and-a-half per cent. Turning to the Minister of Lands, the President queried, "Is that so?"

"No, Sir, I'm afraid it's not as much as that. Perhaps not more than two per cent."

The President turned again to the Minister of Lands and said, "I want you to double the planting programme next year."

I ventured to suggest he might have some difficulty in doing this as many of his trained planters were coming over to help with forestry in England because they were getting such poor wages at home.

"Double their wages," said the President. From then on a progressive forestry policy was adopted and the forestry situation in Eire was thus saved.

Nineteen-forty-seven also proved to be one of the most significant years in the history of the Men of the Trees for it was at the General Meeting in the Chelsea Physic Garden that they assumed world leadership in earth-wide regeneration, launching the new Earth Charter which was translated into most languages with the co-operation of Esperantists.

It was at this time I reminded the Colonial Office that I still worked for them. With the expense of a young family and the growing demands being made upon me by the Men of the Trees, and no pension, it was necessary for me to seek some form of remuneration. The Colonial Office introduced me to the Central Office of Information who invited me to join their headquarters lecture staff, for they were needing people with African experience to meet the growing demand for lectures throughout the country. The work occupied about five days a week and I would fill as many as three or four engagements a day. My transport was arranged from the government pool and I drew upon their green-uniformed drivers. I was able to get back to the farm on Fridays and tackle the Men of the Trees' correspondence. As far as possible I fitted my forest advisory work in with my lecture programme. In the course of three years I had addressed all the principal Rotary Clubs in the United Kingdom, Co-operative Societies, Women's Luncheon Clubs, and a wide cross-section of principal schools and universities. On one occasion a sedate chairman introduced me to a large audience as "the Founder of a Society of Free Lovers"! It was not the first nor the last time that this amusing, if slightly embarrassing slip was made.

Exeter University was chosen for the Summer School the following year, 1948. Professor Caldwell personally conducted us round his arboretum and showed us his famous Luccombe oaks which had originated at Mamhead Park from a cross between *quercus ceris*, the turkey oak, and *quercus suber*, the cork oak. At that time, Mr. Luccombe was head gardener at Mamhead Park. It was with special interest that the Summer School examined the original parent trees on the beautiful estate of our late President. Members also long remembered their interesting visit to Budleigh Salterton, the property of Lord Clinton, for many years a valued member of our Council.

With the help of my old forestry pupil and colleague, Henry Finlayson, I drew up the New Earth Charter and presented it to progressive leaders and functionaries at the New Earth Vegetarian Luncheon held at the De Vere Hotel in Kensington. For three successive years I invited suggestions for modification or additions but it remained unaltered.

Finlayson often told me about his remarkable Austrian acquaintance, Viktor Schauberger, a forester and natural philosopher who was leading a new departure towards a creative economy and whose son, Walter, was chief designer for the Luftwaffe. He designed the first jet fighter plane in collaboration with his father who had discovered the best angle for the baffles from watching the angles of the fins of trout in swift-running streams. I was curious to get more information from this source and persuaded Finlayson to go over to Austria and renew his contact with the Schaubergers.

In 1951 I invited Walter Schauberger to visit England and demonstrate his father's findings in front of professors from Oxford, Cambridge, Birmingham, the Royal Society and Members of the Court of St. James from thirty countries. Professor Bentley, Scientific Adviser to the Admiralty, was also in attendance.

Walter Schauberger's field of research seemed so far in advance of current thought and the old mathematics that only the most advanced physicists could comprehend his direction. A new vocabulary would have to be evolved before this departure could be properly understood. Not being sufficiently advanced in the latest studies of physics and pure mathematics I did not enter into the discussions but I watched Schauberger's demonstrations with keen interest and was impressed by the impact that they made on the more learned scientists in his audience.

Nineteen-fifty-two was marked by my Continental tour in the spring, when I addressed Biological Conferences in Germany and Austria, and gave many broadcasts in support of the Green Front against the threatening deserts. The Germans were gravely concerned about the inroads that had been made into their forests by the French, who took timber to pay indemnities. Forest working plans were entirely ignored and clear felling became the order of the day, with disastrous biological consequences.

The Austrian forests were threatened by the establishment of five great paper mills, erected with Marshall Aid. These mills had far too great an output for a small country like Austria and very soon the forests that had protected the mountains from time immemorial were swept into the digesters of the great pulp mills. Their Minister of Agriculture had been taken to the U.S.A. on a "tour of instruction". He had been presented with a high-powered American car and had returned to do the bidding of his new masters, closing his eyes to the devastation taking place. When I spoke to him about the situation he explained that Austria had to pay interest to America on the loans and this would necessitate increasing exploitation of the forests and other raw materials. With the Iron Curtain in front of them and American and French tanks behind them, the Austrians felt that they were in a parlous plight. The tendency was for them to live for the moment and drown their distress with cocktail parties.

Realizing their desperate position I felt it was essential to work for peace and liberation. I was invited to give a lecture in Vienna to the University graduates. About six hundred turned up. The President had presided at a lecture I had given to the Agricultural College in Vienna, twenty-seven years before when I had taken a party of forestry students from Oxford to visit the forests of Czechoslovakia, Austria and Germany. This time my subject was "Among the Trees of the World", illustrated with original hand-coloured slides from my tree studies. After showing pictures of the redwoods, eucalyptus and the giant kauris of New Zealand I threw a picture on the screen of the giant tree ferns growing up to the edge of the Franz Joseph Glacier. I paused, then continued:

"In good Franz Joseph's day there were twenty-four nations living happily, side by side in your historic capital, while now there are only four—living unhappily. Yet since my arrival in Vienna I have had a feeling that not twenty-four but fifty-four nations could find a spiritual home here.

"I dreamt last night that Winston Churchill rang up President Truman to say, 'We've run out of scrap iron, so I'm afraid we can't go on making munitions for you.'

" 'That's too bad,' said Truman. 'Can't you think of something, big boy?'

" 'Yes,' said Churchill, 'let's scrap the Iron Curtain.'

" 'That's all right with me,' said Truman, 'as long as you put something else in its place.'

" 'We'll put up a Wooden Curtain,' said Churchill.

" 'No you don't,' said Truman. 'What do you think we gave that Marshall Aid for? Don't you know that one metropolitan edition of our newspapers takes three hundred and thirty acres of Canadian forest every time it is printed? We'll soon be falling back on the Austrian forests. Think of something else, bright boy.'

" 'I've got an idea,' said Churchill. 'We'll put up a Glass Curtain. They have wonderful glass in Austria and Czechoslovakia—we'll put up a Glass Curtain!'

"So in my dream up went a sound-proof Glass Curtain. Immediately enterprising New York travel agencies chartered hundreds of planes and brought over thousands of American tourists. In my dream I could see them peering through the Glass Curtain with those wonderful Zeiss binoculars which they were hiring for an Austrian schilling a minute. And what do you think they saw? Earnest-looking people addressing large audiences of school-children. From their serious expressions they appeared to be school-teachers! And soon thousands of children returned to their schools and brought out millions of little trees and planted them and the American tourists could see for themselves great green belts of trees stretching away into the distance. The tourists returned to their country and went to their President and said, 'We've got to get the help of these Russian boys and girls to fix our Dust Bowl.' And then I woke up!

"Is it too much to hope," I continued, "that the Iron Curtains of the world will give place to the Green Front and the scars in the earth as well as the scars in people's hearts may be healed by tree-planting? As the Persian seer declared, 'This is the hour of the coming together of the sons of men. The earth will indeed become as a Garden and a Paradise.' I truly believe that 'the leaves of the Tree will be for the healing of the Nations'."

I closed on that note. My chairman concluded the meeting with undisguised emotion and people rushed up to me to thank me. Foremost was an Austrian Count who embraced me affectionately, kissed me on both cheeks, saying,

"You've done something for us, you've lifted a great weight. You've given us something to live for. I want to talk to you. Do come to dinner."

I explained that I had about seventeen supporters with me and Austrian members of the Men of the Trees. He said,

"Bring them with you, we have plenty of cars."

He proved to be one of the largest forest landowners in the country. His only child, a daughter, was married to a forest engineer who was supervising his woodlands and he was paying an Austrian forestry professor a retaining fee to prepare and supervise forest working plans. The Count invited me to stay with him. After a few days there, I decided that this would be an ideal training-ground for students from the University of the Sahara and the Count agreed to take up to thirty for six months a year.

The following day I was continuing my journey in the mountains of Austria when I met a professor who had been deploring the establishment of destructive paper mills and had warned the authorities of the risk entailed. He had become a thorn in the side of the ruthless exploiters; to get rid of him they had offered him a professorship in the U.S. A. This he politely declined as he felt his duty was to educate his own people. He seemed to be just the man I needed to train my Sahara students. He willingly consented to be the first Dean of the University of the Sahara, unpaid, and to take charge of thirty students for six months in the year.

The idea of conservation won through. Three of the paper mills worked themselves to a standstill, giving the conservationists a chance to step up their planting programme. Nevertheless, much damage had already been done and avalanches destroyed many villages, lives and property, and later floods caused much devastation and loss of life.

I returned to London in time for the Annual World Forestry Charter Gathering at the Dorchester on March 21, and reported to ambassadors from about fifty countries, enlisting support for the Green Front.

Chapter 8

THE EVER-EXPANDING WORK OF THE MEN OF THE TREES

Outside my walled garden
There lies a desert land
Nor tree, nor bird, nor blossom
But only sky and sand.
Wild in the hot sirocco
The whirling dust is blown;
Yet there I'll set my kingdom
There will I rear my throne.

Contributed M.G.
(By kind permission—NORAH M. HOLLAND
The Macmillan Company—1924)

URING MY VISIT to Germany I had enlisted the help of Dr. Schenk, who had become a member of the Men of the Trees. Many years before, he had been invited by the American Government to open the first forestry school in the U.S.A. Generations of American foresters had been trained by him. During World War I he was sent back to Germany with no funds and without a pension, simply because of his nationality. His old students felt that this was unjust and wished that they could persuade their Government to make amends. Individually many of them had sent parcels and gifts and kept in touch with him through those difficult years. Now they decided that the time had come to have a reunion of the Biltmorians and they invited the old professor to unveil a monument to the school. Dr. Schenk had been greatly looking forward to renewing past friendships but on the eve of his departure his aged wife became ill and he was unable to leave her. He telephoned me in Dorset, asking me to take his place and represent him and European foresters at the first reunion of the Biltmore Forestry School.

Leaving Finlayson in charge of headquarters I flew to New York. On my arrival there I found newspaper correspondents waiting to interview me. There had been a four-and-a-half-month drought and

New York had run short of water. In desperation the City fathers had sent up planes to seed the clouds in the hope of inducing rain in the vicinity. I was asked by the Press what I thought of this and why, in my opinion, New York was so short of water. I expressed the view that their water shortage was the result of deforestation and it was a short-sighted policy to expect to get water for the city by seeding the clouds.

This interview gave me the opportunity to present the New Earth Charter to the Americans and I went on my way via Washington and Ashville to Biltmore. The following day I joined the Biltmorians in an expedition to the site of the old forest school on the Vanderbilt estate and was guest speaker at their reunion dinner. I was also given an Honorary Degree in Forestry and made a Life Member of their alumni.

Perhaps it was significant that immediately preceding my visit to Ashville in North Carolina, there had been a big "blow" for three-and-a-half days, when the soil was lifted from seven States in the south-west and deposited in the Atlantic. Farmers sat in their shacks actually counting the farms as they were blown away, guessing to whom they belonged. They would point jokingly to a black cloud and say: "Boys, did you see my farm go by?" It was strange to me that the United States were spending more money on education in soil conservation than any country in the world and they had one of the finest soil conservation services.

On my return to New York I was welcomed again on the air by Lowell Thomas who gave me an all too short three-and-a-half minutes to bring home to the American people the urgency of tackling their dustbowl problem which seemed to be reaching Saharan dimensions.

It was in the autumn of 1952, with the blessing of the Universities of Vienna, Sorbonne, Oxford and Cambridge, that I was privileged to lead the First Sahara University Expedition. The object was to carry out an ecological line survey across the Sahara and along the Equator to estimate the speed at which the Sahara was advancing on the few remaining food-bearing lands along the southern perimeter. In the spring of the same year I attended the Biological Conferences in Austria and on my return to London gave a luncheon at the Dorchester, Park Lane, to members of the

Court of St. James from thirty-two countries who supported my proclamation of a green army against the deserts. After that I set out, accompanied by Audley Money-Kyrle, who had just taken a degree in Ecology at Trinity, and Ray Perry, an artist, ornithologist and a dowser. He had worked for the Forestry Commission in Wales and was dedicated to Sahara Reclamation. He determined to spend the rest of his life on this project.

I had been terrified by reports coming in from F.A.O. and U.N.E.S.C.O. Conferences, indicating the speed at which the deserts of the world were advancing. This news helped to create interest for a fact-finding expedition across the Sahara.

To raise funds to buy petrol I wrote *Famous Trees* for Lord Kemsley's Dropmore Press. In his review for *Country Life*, which appeared when I was in the Sahara, Howard Spring wrote: "What with the fine binding, the deckled, handmade paper, the satisfying type and the drawings by S. R. Badmin, the Dropmore Press has presented Mr. Richard St. Barbe Baker's *Famous Trees* in a way no author could complain of."

The book sold for two guineas a copy and there were fifty copies even more sumptuous at a more sumptuous price. It was given the National Book Society's Award for one of the Twelve Best Books of the year, and the advance payment I received was invaluable in financing the Expedition.

During the following months preparations went ahead and I recruited a team to accompany me. None of us had much to lose, least of all myself. My home had become unhappy and my marriage was in the process of being legally dissolved. One other member of my team was also broken-hearted and a third had been threatened by loss of sight.

I acquired a secondhand Desert Humber from the Government Disposals Board; it had a reconditioned engine and cost me £350. My friends protested about my using an old war vehicle. "It's all very well for you," they said, "if you want to commit suicide that way, but it is not fair to take these young people with you." However, they had made the decision themselves and were keen to set out as soon as possible. We had the backing of the Annual General Meeting of the Men of the Trees and the members of the Summer School at Harrogate.

On the Saturday night prior to our departure I was interviewed on television on *In Town Tonight*. After introducing the subject of our proposed Expedition to Nairobi by way of the Sahara, I mentioned that two days previously one of our members reported that he had picked five hundred peaches from a tree raised from a stone he had sown five years before. I appealed to viewers for peach stones that I could take as a gesture from the heart of London to the heart of the Sahara and said that we would be attending a dedication service at St. Martin-in-the-Field at noon the following Tuesday.

When I came out from St. Martin's I found members and friends from many parts of England looking for the Expedition van so that they could deliver parcels of peach stones. There was a postman too with packages of peach stones who was relieved to find we would accept them. Barrow-boys were doing a roaring trade selling peaches and friends up from the country were buying peaches and presenting them to us. Throughout the lunch period we ate peaches, depositing the stones in a sack held by Gordon Vokes, who had fitted the Expedition car with his famous sand filters. The sack was soon filled to overflowing and we left Trafalgar Square on the first leg of the long trek, which took us as far as the Dover Cliffs Hotel that night. There we were given a farewell by members who had arrived independently.

Before leaving England we had visited the French Consulate to ask permission for our expedition to cross the Sahara. It was flatly refused, with the words: "Haven't you seen the papers lately? Only three weeks ago three professors set out in a jeep and after three days they were missing. We sent out three French Officers in another jeep to look for them and after five days' fruitless search they too were missing. We then sent up a plane to look for both parties and it drew blank and now we've sent out camels. What we want to know is: who is going to pay for the camels?" However, as we said goodbye to our friends we decided that we must get as far as Paris at least and tackle the Colonial Office there.

On our arrival in France we found the peach stone story was making headlines. One French professor was protesting that peaches would not grow in the Sahara and another professor was equally emphatic that only recently he had picked some beautiful peaches growing at Tamanrasset, right in the heart of the Sahara.

When we reached Paris we renewed our efforts to obtain permission for our desert crossing and spent a fruitless morning waiting at the French Colonial Office. Just before noon the man we wished to see came down and expressed his regrets at keeping us waiting so long. He invited us to lunch to discuss the matter. After lunch he said the matter was out of his province and that we must apply to the General Officer Commanding the Sahara. By this time it was too late to make an appointment that afternoon; however, we were promised one the next day. It was not until almost noon that the General consented to see us and, apologizing for the delay, wafted us off to lunch, explaining that it was quite impossible for him to give permission: however, he insisted upon feeding us.

That afternoon we called on the Agent General for Algeria, who had been a prisoner of war and was a poet. Sensing my earnestness, he inquired: "Do you need permission?" So taking his hint we set out—with French leave!

We had been thoughtfully equipped by Group Captain Douglas Thompson with a compact suitcase containing a signalling outfit, such as was used in underground movements during the war. We were to get code signals to enable us to keep in touch with the administrators of the Sahara. As we had officially been refused permission for our journey, naturally code signals were not provided. So when we finally left the Algerian frontier we left all contact behind us.

The 2,600-mile desert crossing and journey on to Kilimanjaro proved to be one of the most exhilarating experiences of my life. My book, *Sahara Challenge*, describes the nine thousand miles we drove, sleeping under the stars. We had many narrow escapes from death and were constantly reminded of our possible fate by that of others—sometimes all that remained of a hopeful driver was a shin bone sticking out of an old shoe! We were not terrified so much by the speed at which we glided over the hard-packed sand with a little finger touching the wheel to keep general direction, when a heavier hand would have caused a somersault and burst tyres, or the engulfing quicksands or dried-out river beds, but by the speed at which we found the desert encroaching on the few remaining areas of fertile lands.

Passing through the Congo we had heard from American missionaries that all the Chiefs in Kenya had been murdered or shot during the emergency which had recently been declared.

"Not Josiah," I exclaimed involuntarily, and then realized that they had had the latest news from their colleagues in Kenya. On my arrival in Nairobi I was greeted by one of the old forest guards who relieved my anxiety about Josiah, assuring me that he was safe. That evening I drove out to Kibichiku, Chief Josiah's farm, and found him safe and sound, and warmly welcoming after my long absence since 1923. He knew that his life was threatened every night. The report that I had received from the Congo missionaries was true, for all the other Kikuyu Chiefs had been either shot or murdered. My old friend gave me his own bed and, pointing to a gun leaning against the wall, said, "It's loaded."

"I don't need it, Josiah, thank you," I said. "I have a secret weapon, I'll tell you about it sometime."

"I'll give it back to James," he said. He had borrowed it from his farmer son especially for me. That night I went to sleep after listening to one of my favourite records, the Canoe Song, by Paul Robeson from *Sanders of the River*, which ends, "And each for all and all for each until we reach the journey's end."

It was a sad country to which I had returned, deeply contrasting with the happy days when I had started the Dance of the Trees. I had looked forward with excitement to my return and had even pictured a reunion of thousands of Kikuyu under the sacred Mugumu Tree where candidates had been initiated into the Tree Planting Brotherhood, but there was no more song and dance now. Once as I drove along the road to Nairobi I came upon a group of Kikuyu, who ran away and hid. I had never experienced anything like this before. Stopping the car I got out and called them to me.

"*Endo haha, endone*"—"Come here, come." Slowly they emerged from their hiding place, still suspicious. However, I coaxed them towards me and assured them that I was their old friend, the Bab wa Miti. Their eyes opened wide with wonder and they were grateful for the lift I gave them to Nairobi. That evening a law was passed making it illegal for anybody to give Kikuyu lifts on the road. I spent what little money I had in buying corn from the Indian stocks but it was hopeless to attempt to feed a million Kikuyu on the verge of starvation.

They had been crowded down into the Kikuyu Land Unit with no money and no food. There they met their fellows in the same plight; with no work and no food they would go up into the forest to live as they might on roots of trees or anything they could find in the way of sustenance. Much as I would like to have stayed amongst my old friends I felt that I could be of better service to them back in England, negotiating with the Colonial Office and members of the Houses of Commons and Lords.

Jomo Kenyatta was on trial. He had been sent to me, so many years before, by the Wa Kamba to speak to England's King on their behalf. I had been in my office at the London headquarters of the Men of the Trees when the telephone rang. Miss Foster, one of the secretaries, answered it and, turning to me, said: "There's somebody talking, probably in an African dialect. Perhaps you would take the call."

It was Kenyatta, asking for the Baba wa Miti. "Where are you speaking from?" I inquired, in his own language.

He explained that he was at Piccadilly Circus. I told him to stay by the telephone box and I would come and fetch him. I brought him back with me to the office where he told me how their cattle were being commandeered and sold to the American canning factory—steers for five shillings, calves for one shilling. They were being auctioned, but there was only one buyer. The chief and elders had appealed to the Governor and presented him with a petition begging him to stop taking their cattle. The petition was beautifully typed, and he had with him certified copies of it. I contacted Malcolm MacDonald, the Colonial Secretary, who arranged for me to see the Senior Clerk at the Colonial Office on behalf of my African friends.

Now Jomo Kenyatta was on trial for his life. The trial had become a morning show for the settlers' wives who were curious to see which colour jacket he would wear! He was eventually condemned on false witness and carried away in chains. It was not until years later that the witness admitted that there was no truth in his statement. He had been bribed by the police and, needing the money for his family, was unable to resist the temptation.

I still had one important engagement in Kampala where I had been entrusted by Shoghi Effendi, the Guardian of the Baha'i Cause, to act as host to the African believers who were attending the first Intercontinental Teaching Conference. My first duty each morning was to take the caterer to the market to buy provisions for the day. Then I had to collect the African delegates from the club where they were staying and take them to the Conference. In the evening I took them back again. It took several trips even though I could crowd eighteen or twenty on to the Desert Humber.

One evening, returning for the last time, I stopped at a garage for a few minutes. When I came out, the car had gone. I said to the garage man: "What's happened to my car?"

"Your car? I haven't seen one," he said.

"But I left it there only a few minutes ago."

"You should have brought it into the garage, not left it by the side of the road. Someone's taken it," he said.

I went to the nearest police station and reported what had happened. The police officer seemed quite unconcerned and told me that it was the fifth car that had been reported stolen that evening.

"You might do something about it," I suggested. "Here is the number and description. I've driven this car across the Sahara and it's very valuable to me."

"Trouble is," said the policeman, "they knock them apart in the night and distribute the spare parts so you have little chance of seeing it again. It's become a big business these days. However, I will alert the other station."

I gave him my telephone number and, wishing him luck, said I would await his news. I got into a taxi and went to the Bahá'í Hazeras and Conference Headquarters where I told my friends about the theft. It seemed so unfair to me that when I was doing my best to help the cause this should have happened. One of the Persian Bahá'í's suggested that we should pray—"Is there any Remover of Difficulties, save God . . ."—and this we did, saying the prayer nine times. Shortly afterwards, the telephone rang and the police reported that my car had been found, about thirty miles out of town, and unharmed. I congratulated them. This was good news indeed and it seemed a direct answer. Before many minutes had elapsed the telephone rang again and a police officer explained that the two officers who had retrieved the car had gone into an inn to celebrate and when they had come out they found that the two policemen they had left in charge of the car had been knocked on the head, thrown in a ditch and the car had gone again. I reported this to my Bahá'í friends who once again suggested prayer. In the morning a member of the Conference Committee beckoned me to the corner of the road and said: "You haven't by any chance lost a Sahara car, have you?"

There was the old Humber, apparently none the worse for the night's outing! The police told me to leave it untouched so that they might get fingerprints, but I explained that I had already been handling it and thanked them for their trouble.

This first Intercontinental Teaching Conference had come at a time when the whole of Equatorial Africa was in ferment. Heads of the Cause and delegates were met at the airport by the African believers, who greeted them with an embrace. This was the first time that anything like this had happened and it did much to relieve the unhappy situation.

Before finally departing I called on Sir Evelyn Baring, who was in conference with the Governors of Tanganyika and Uganda, and presented them each with one of Esselmont's books, entitled *Bahá'u'lláh and the New Era*, explaining to them the contribution that the Bahá'í Cause could make to administration in Africa. As he walked with me to the Conference room, Sir Evelyn said: "By the way, Baker, your plan for employing detainees in forestry camps is coming off."

I left my car on loan to the caterer, a Madagascan and with a sense of deep satisfaction boarded the plane for London.

One of my first engagements was the Eighth World Forestry Charter Gathering, where I reported to diplomatic representatives of forty-four countries. During the next few weeks I was busily engaged in writing my reports and my book, *Sahara Challenge*, proofs of which were ready to submit to the next World Forestry Charter Gathering, in 1954.

I have always felt that one of the most interesting institutions in Great Britain is the platform for campaigners and their causes at Speakers' Corner. When I got back from my first Sahara University Expedition I could not wait for my organized lectures, and so on the first Sunday morning I took my banner with "JOIN THE GREEN FRONT" on it to Speakers' Corner where I set up my platform between the two largest audiences; the Catholics were to the right of me and the Communists to the left. Soon curiosity was aroused and people gathered around as I warmed up to my subject.

It was not long before an experienced trouble-maker butted in and tried to shout me down, whereupon I invited him to my platform saying I wanted to give him a sporting chance of being heard. He was somewhat taken aback but I insisted that he take my place and when he had had his say, which lasted less than a minute, I resumed my platform, and soon about a couple of hundred were sufficiently interested to stand and listen. I asked my audience what they would do if they had seen for themselves the oncoming desert threatening the lives of the people. I cited the instance of old French West Africa to the north of Ghana where, seeing the end of the forest in sight with hundreds of miles of desert in front of them to the south and the wilderness closing in on them from the north, chiefs had forbidden marriage and women refused to bear children, for they would raise them for certain starvation.

Among the hecklers I found some quite good speakers but managed to win them over. After only a few Sundays several of them were quite in a position to take over from me, and when I had to be away I entrusted one with my banner. Three Sundays later as I happened to be passing through London, I visited my old stand and there was a man who had been one of the worst trouble-makers, pounding out the gospel of tree-planting, talking about transpiration and how trees created a micro-climate and so on. Unobserved I crept up behind him and listened, fascinated by his eloquence, now being used constructively, and by the grip he had of my subject.

Our Summer School in 1953, the year that I returned from leading the first Sahara University Expedition, was centred on Inverness under the Chairmanship of Lord Sempill, who for so long had been my strong supporter, often presiding at the World Forestry Charter Gatherings I had held annually at the Dorchester, Park Lane.

Here in his native land, among the trees, he was very much at home and took us to many interesting estates where the Scottish lairds were as enthusiastic as he was about trees. At the conclusion of this memorable Summer School, during which we were honoured by a visit from Queen Elizabeth, the Queen Mother, I stayed with him at his home, Craigie Castle. For days we visited estates where trees had suffered as a result of the storm on January 31 that year, when a freezing wind had blown for eight hours, uprooting eleven million trees.

We inspected the tree-roots to read if possible the cause of this disaster. We found that most of the trees felled in the storm were approximately forty years of age when root competition had become severe. It is a fact that the hair roots of pines are charged with an acid sheath; nature has provided this to help dissolve rocks and enable the root to penetrate. One often sees how the tiny root of a pine, by the sheer force of expansion, has succeeded in splitting a rock, emerging a foot or so below the point of entry. Imagine myriads of small roots competing with each other at the same level for growing space. When this happens an acid pan is formed at the level of the greatest root competition. For the health of pines there must be a mixture of broad-leaved trees so that the leaf-fall can provide food for the roots of the conifers. Nature is wonderful in her adaptations for she provides a symbiotic fungus whose strands attach themselves at one end to the decaying leaf of the hardwood tree while the other end contacts the tiny feeding roots of the pine. This process is known as a micorrhizal association. It was the outside trees of the plantations which had remained standing while those inside were uprooted by the storm. This was because the trees on the outside enjoyed this micorrhizal association which arose from the leaves of the hedges and other non-coniferous plants and shrubs. In the natural forest there is a mixture of broad-leaved trees and when a pine forest is felled, silver birch, whose catkins are carried far in the wind, are the first to take root. In due course pines appear here and there and push their way up among the light-demanding silver birches and eventually suppress them. The silver birch is a natural nurse tree and has a retiring disposition, giving place to the more important species it nurses. The Men of the Trees have continually urged the importance of mixed forests and the value of planting poplar as a fireguard around coniferous woods.

Going on to Rothiemurchass, where I stayed with Colonel Iain Grant, an enthusiastic member of the Men of the Trees and a most successful landowner, I found that the natural Caledonian forest with pines and silver birch had stood up to the storm and it was quite an exception to find a fallen tree.

While I was on the Sahara expedition, the great elms of Kensington Broad Walk were felled, much to the distress of the residents. We found that another four thousand elms were threatened in Hyde Park. The Men of the Trees were urged to call a meeting in Kensington Town Hall to protest; about eight hundred people turned up. Lord Sempill presided and among the speakers were Sir John Eden, Nancy Price, Sir Shane Leslie, and an old lady who had lived all her life in the vicinity of the Broad Walk. Sir John spoke first and was followed by Nancy Price, who had just got up from a sick-bed to be present. She made an impassioned appeal, at the close of which she had to return to her bed. Sir Shane was the next speaker. He reminded the audience that in Ireland the shillelagh was a valuable weapon and he advised the people of Kensington to take a hint from the Irish when their trees were threatened! When my turn came, I reported that I had examined every felled elm and found them in good health. True, there were three with hollows in them but they were healthy and still growing. I told the story of a past Minister of Works who had gone to King Edward, the Peacemaker, and reported:

"Sir, there are three hollow trees in your Broad Walk. I must fell them."

Said the King, "You do not fell a single elm in the Broad Walk. If you did so, I might lose my Crown, my people love them too well."

I asked whether our Queen had been consulted before her trees had been felled.

"That is what the people of Kensington want to know. Was it

a coincidence," I asked, "that these trees were razed to the ground while Her Majesty was on the other side of the world in New Zealand?"

These trees were reported to have been attacked by the elm disease and supposed to be dangerous. Some people seemed to think just because a tree was hollow it was dangerous. The hollow mast of a racing yacht was not dangerous because it was hollow, and as long as these trees were growing, adding layer upon layer of wood, they could not be said to be dangerous. I suggested that the Minister had been ill-advised. Pressure might have been brought to bear by the timber market, owing to the shortage of coffin wood resulting from the increasing number of motor accidents. Perhaps people should drive more carefully to protect their elms! I proposed that the meeting should appoint a deputation to wait on the Minister of Works and insist that a tree committee be formed to advise him before any further elms were felled in the London parks. The proposal was accepted and Lord Sempill, Sir Shane Leslie and myself were appointed to take the petition to the Minister forthwith. We also obtained the backing of Sir Arthur Bryant, who put in a word for the elms in his page in *The Illustrated London News*, and spoke elsewhere on their behalf.

One of the members of my club who was always vigilant for the trees, told me that his daughter was taking her dog for a walk that very morning when she saw a Park keeper taking time off from collecting waste paper on the end of a stick to put white crosses on the trunks of some of the finest of the elms. The girl inquired:

"What do those crosses mean?"

"They've got to come down," he said.

"But those are beautiful trees. You mustn't cut those down," said the girl. Whereupon he started to erase the marks and put crosses on others. To a Man of the Trees it was a tragedy that such an irresponsible person should be at large among the glorious trees of Hyde Park.

I am glad to say that our deputation was so effective that the Minister of Works was promoted to be Minister of Education and the trees were saved. This was a good year indeed for the Men of the Trees. Already the Sahara University Expedition had considerably strengthened their membership and the added publicity over the Broad Walk elms attracted many more people.

Exactly two years after leaving on the Sahara Expedition I set out once more, this time for New Zealand at the invitation of the Men of the Trees there and the farmers and fruit-growers of Central Otago, who were needing advice on the establishment of shelter belts. They had asked the State Forestry Service what to plant and were told that trees would not grow in Central Otago and that even if they succeeded they would not pay. One of our members, Dr. Fitzgerald, who had read some of my books and who had followed our expedition in the Sahara, thought that the man who could make trees grow in the Sahara would be able to make them grow even in Central Otago. He and a neighbouring tree enthusiast, Philip Barling, cabled me inviting me to come out and advise them. As my dear mother was in her ninety-sixth year, I felt I could not leave her then. However, they sent Gerald Fergusson of Dunedin as deputy. He arrived at the Annual General Meeting of the Men of the Trees at Chelsea Physic Gardens and appealed to my Council to spare me. They at once agreed and my mother was insistent that I should go. She assured me that she was well cared-for by faithful retainers.

I sailed on the *Rangitani* and amused myself by entertaining the seventy-five children on board, relieving their parents for an hour each evening. My bed-time stories proved popular and a young compère introduced me each night.

At Wellington I was met by Philip Barling and Chev Bell, who had been my sergeant in King Edward's Horse. I was given a Mayoral Reception and Heads of Departments and the City Fathers were presented to me. His Worship the Mayor referred to my previous visit, twenty-three years before, when I had prepared plans which were now resulting in returns of twelve million pounds a year. In my reply I requested that a tree be planted along the new road between Auckland and Wellington for each of my young fellow passengers and that in future a tree should be planted for each young New Zealander whether he or she arrived by sea, air, or stork!

Philip Barling was anxious to take me back with him to Glen-falloch and I arrived there to find his beautiful gardens gay with spring blossoms. He proved to be a wonderful host and arranged a full programme of lectures and advisory work for me. Each weekend I returned to Glenfalloch and its beautiful trees and gardens for rest and inspiration. It was there at a garden party given in my honour that I met Catriona Burnett and her mother, from Mt. Cook. I fell for them both at first sight and invited them to come and stay with me in England. One weekend at Glenfalloch I heard that my dear mother had fallen, broken her thigh and gone into the Southampton Hospital to have it pinned. The next cable reported that the operation had been successful and that she was making a good recovery. Somewhat relieved I set out to Central Otago for my big meeting to form a branch of the Men of the Trees and, if possible, to get the Government to launch some sort of Farm Forestry Programme. It was an impressive meeting. Farmers came from far and near and a Committee with Chairman and Secretary was elected. The Mayor of Alexandra had arranged a reception at his beautiful home and the Mayor of Roxborough joined in. Afterwards, the newly elected Chairman, Councillor Barrett and Trevor Ross, who had been driving me all day, took me to the little hotel where I was their guest. They brought me to my room to make quite sure that I had everything I required. I thanked them for the splendid arrangements and for their kindness.

Then Barrett said that a cable had come for me at four o'clock that afternoon but they had held it for me till now, as I had had such a full programme. It was from my brother, Scott, to say that our mother's operation had been entirely successful but that she had been taken from us that morning. As the eldest of the family I would dearly have loved to have been at her side, but in Central Otago I could not have been much further away.

That night I could not sleep and chided myself that if only I had been at home with her the accident might not have happened. I recalled her generous insistence that if the people of New Zealand needed me I must answer their call. I thought of her wonderful life of sacrifice for others and how she would be missed by her neighbours and friends. I thought of her thousands of old Sunday School scholars throughout the Dominions who would be grieving at the news of her passing, and prayed that I might be worthy of her trust and faith in me and my work for our fellow-men and the Men of the Trees everywhere. I thought how often the inauguration of a new, constructive idea exacted the sacrifice of a life and how willingly my dear mother would have surrendered her life if only her son's work might be blessed for future generations by New Zealanders. That night I rededicated my life to the cause of the Men of the Trees and to creating a tree sense in the rising generation.

Realizing that the gardeners and other old friends at The Firs would be anxious about their future, I decided to return to Southampton on the same boat that had brought me out. After our exhibition in the War Memorial Museum at Auckland of Lonsdale Ragg's drawings and my own tree photographs, enlarged from studies I had specially selected for the *Tree Lovers' Calendar*, I re-embarked on the *Rangitani* and was welcomed by the Captain and Officers. A comfortable single cabin had been reserved for me and I was able to start writing *Land of Tané*, Erosion in New Zealand, a report of my findings during my recent tour of both islands, with recommendations as regards conservation and restoring the natural tree cover.

In a most kind and generous foreword, Viscount Bledisloe, a late Governor-General of New Zealand wrote:

"Richard St. Barbe Baker has earned for himself the reputation of being the greatest living authority in the English-speaking world on the supreme value of silviculture from the standpoint alike of scenic beauty, economic importance, dominant climatic influence, and human health. He is a man of wide knowledge, exceptional culture, and penetrating vision."

Here indeed was something to live up to. A fellow-passenger very kindly typed my chapters and this was done in record time. Then I began another book, *Horse Sense—The Story of my Horses in War and Peace*, dedicated to my children Angela and Paul who also loved horses. In addition to my writing I gave lectures on "Trees and Travel", and, as before, devoted myself for an hour each evening to the children; and so the voyage was a full and happy one.

For two or three days before we docked I was frequently cornered by a child who would whisper in my ear, "Shall I tell you a secret?", or "Don't tell anybody but you are going to have a surprise!"

On the last evening of the voyage the children gathered round with much excitement and presented me with a beautifully wrapped parcel. They were agog to see me open it. As I continued to admire it their impatience mounted. Finally I called for the person who was responsible for the beautiful packing. A shy little girl approached and between us, very slowly, we unwrapped the parcel. A carved box was disclosed. This in turn I admired, while they all shouted: "Open it, open it!"

Realizing it was a musical box I continued to tantalize my excited audience by opening the box a mere fraction of an inch and closing it again with a snap. When I could resist their clamour no longer, I opened it wide and it played a Swiss Mountain Air, to the delight and relief of everyone present.

I went back to my old home, The Firs, and did my best to keep things going, carrying on the family traditions with as little change as possible.

During the war I had kept in touch with my family, and after my father's death contrived to visit my old home at least once every ten days or so. The oldest gardener, Harry Davis, had been in the service of the family for sixty-four years and I submitted his name to the Royal Horticultural Society for their Gold Medal for long service. On one of these occasions I asked Harry if all was well and whether there were any complaints. His usual reply was to the effect that they were "rubbing along" or everything was "fair to middlin' ", but on this particular occasion he drew a long face and replied: "Yes, sir, I have a complaint."

My reaction was to ask him to tell me the worst, to which he replied: "Fifty-two years ago today, sir, your father said to me, 'Harry, what about coming round for a week's trial?' That was fifty-two years ago today, sir, and nobody's told me whether I have given satisfaction or not."

"Surely, Harry," I said, "you know in your heart whether you have given satisfaction, or not. You don't need me to tell you that."

At this point William Line, the foreman, who had overheard our conversation, came a few steps nearer and said: "It's all very well for Harry to be boasting how long he's been with us, but come next Christmas I will have been here fifty-two years too."

"Harry, William, that's marvellous," said I. "Do you know what my dear father would have said if he had been here? 'Harry, William, you each deserve a gold watch as big as a frying pan.' And so you do and we must celebrate."

Some time later, during the middle of the strawberry season, I threw a tea-party and got Southampton caterers to put on a strawberry tea to which I invited all Harry's and William's friends and neighbours. Then I presented each of them with an illuminated address and a purse of money. One can never adequately thank such valued friends for long service.

When the Royal Horticultural Society's Gold Medal arrived, two bars were added. Harry was interviewed by the representative of the *Southern Echo*, who asked, "Mr. Davis, now that you have received this handsome award, I suppose you will be retiring?" To which he replied, "I shall stay with Mr. Baker as long as he needs me." True to his word, he stayed with me until the morning I went to live in New Zealand.

In mid-1952 the Headquarters of the Men of the Trees was transferred to 16 Mulberry Walk, Chelsea, the home of the first Honorary Secretary, Mrs. Grant-Duff. Council meetings had been held there regularly. Now that I was returning to my old home I allowed headquarters to be transferred to The Firs, West End, Southampton, so often referred to as "The Gateway of England". I advertised in the local paper for a secretary, preferably a retired clerk or accountant with executive experience. Within days I had three hundred applications for the job. For the time being I allowed these to accumulate and on the third evening, as I was on my way to the office to start opening them, a letter was slipped into the letter-box in the front door. It dropped on to the mat. Immediately I opened the door and said, "Who is putting letters in my box?" and invited the person inside.

While reading her application and credentials I handed her a copy of *I Planted Trees*. In a few minutes I decided to engage this applicant, Miss Margaret Sims, who had recently come to live with her parents in a neighbouring house. She had only had three positions in her long career as a secretary and each of them had been confidential and responsible. She had also been trained in cartography and lettering which proved to be invaluable in work connected with the *Journal* and our exhibitions. She remained with the Society until our headquarters was moved to the estate of our President, Lord Bessborough, at Stanstead Park, Rowlands Castle, in Hampshire, when Mr. W. C. Browning, His Lordship's secretary, took over the Secretaryship.

The 1955 World Forestry Charter Gathering was again held at the Dorchester. We had a record attendance presided over by Lord Courthope, our President. Assisted by Sir John Eden, I demonstrated the broad outline of my plan to contain and reclaim the two million square miles of the Sahara.

That year the Summer School and Conference was held at Tunbridge Wells and among other estates we had the privilege of visiting our President's at Whiligh, Sussex. Sir Shane Leslie took a leading part and I often called upon him to propose votes of thanks to our many hosts and hostesses. One of the outstanding events was our visit to the country counterpart of Kew Gardens, at Bedgebury, which proved to be most instructive. Here I was put through my paces identifying trees and in turn had fun with the various botanical experts. Somebody argued with me that it was very easy to tell the difference between a swamp cypress, *Taxodium distichum*, and the much advertised Dawn Tree, *Meta sequoia glyptostroboides*. My point was proved when the Director himself slipped up when identifying the bunch of specimens I held in my hand. Before the conclusion of the School we visited the Gordon Clementsons' Happy Valley estate which they had taken over at my suggestion some years before and treescaped most attractively.

In the autumn *Land of Tané* was published. With the help of my old friend, Evelyn Harbord, I wrote *Kabongo* and later *Kamiti — A Forester's Dream*, both published by George Ronald.

I decided to bring the Paris Exhibition, "L'Homme Contre la Nature", to Cambridge to coincide with the next Summer School to be held there, one more at Newnham College. I had twice visited this exhibition in Paris, on my way to the Sahara and on my return, and was anxious that it be sent throughout the world, and that England should give a lead by having it staged in the United Kingdom. I had invited M. Tendron to our New Earth Luncheon on his way to Cambridge to survey the Senate House which I booked as the most worthy building in Britain for this historic exhibition. When I put this proposition to my Council, they fought shy of the expense so I had to bear it myself, as I was convinced of the value of the exhibition. As the fabric of the Senate House had to be untouched, a complete tubular scaffolding had to be designed to support the huge exhibits and enlarged photographs. Eventually two ten-ton truckloads crossed the Channel and drove straight to the Senate House from the port.

The French Minister for Cultural Relations graciously accepted my invitation to open the exhibition and invitations were sent to the Ambassadors, giving them an opportunity of assessing the possibility of introducing this display to their own countries.

"Man Against Nature" was an arresting title and attracted many thinking people and educationalists throughout the country. Yet it failed to bring the masses that it had in Paris. Perhaps Cambridge was too much of a backwater. Despite this I had the satisfaction of hearing from M. Tendron that twelve ambassadors had invited the display to their respective countries. Those attending the Summer School had the advantage of frequently visiting the Senate House and two other exhibitions of tree paintings, both in oils and water-colours, which had been arranged to coincide with "Man Against Nature".

Two of the most memorable expeditions of this Summer School were to the Forestry Commission plantings near Thetford, undertaken as early as 1919, and to Lord Fisher's beautifully wooded estate at Kilveston. Here we were reminded that when the father of the current owner returned from the Governorship of Bombay and found he had three thousand acres at his disposal, he had said, "God made this country for the birds," and had set out to make the best shoot in East Anglia!

From Kilveston Hall we proceeded to Hargham Hall where I had planted Henry's fast-growing poplar in 1919; in 1924 I had advised the owner to plant the same species in poor rush-ridden meadows. The first trees had attained a height of 125 feet and a girth of 125 inches, but the second planting far outstripped them in height.

Many of the trees reached 145 feet or more, though were not pro-
portionately large in circumference because they had been planted
closer together. Looking at these giant trees it seemed hard to
believe that they had all sprung from a little bundle of cuttings
that I had put in my Burberry coat-pocket at the Forestry School
at Cambridge before setting out to prepare a plan of management
for Sir Hugh Beevor at Hargham Hall in December, 1919.

Chapter 9

ON THE BRINK

*Yea, though I walk through the valley of the shadow of death,
I will fear no evil; for Thou art with me; Thy rod and Thy staff
they comfort me.*

Psalm 23:4

I WAS DETERMINED that the Sahara Reclamation Programme
should avoid going headlong into a project before tests had
been carried out in small areas in each of the interested
countries. The abortive ground-nut scheme put me on my guard.

At the outset it was important for us to discover why such an
imaginative scheme had failed. Because Nigerian farmers could
produce so many bushels of ground-nuts in a fraction of an acre,
it was estimated that so many billion bushels could be produced
on so many million acres elsewhere. Batteries of bulldozers were
acquired and chained together to walk away with the bush and
protecting tree cover. Little did the mechanics driving those
machines understand the disaster they were perpetrating. What
did they know of the biological contribution that trees made in
the water cycle, or their vital function in producing rich crops of
ground-nuts year after year, for the Nigerian growers?

From time immemorial it had been the habit of Nigerian farmers
to make little clearings in the high forest where they would sow
the ground-nuts. As the sun rose the areas were shaded by the
surrounding trees. Towards noon the leaves of the ground-nuts
would open out and shade the soil, keeping it cool, and at about
four o'clock the leaves would begin to fold up like butterflies'
wings at rest, allowing the ground to become cool. As the sun
went down the warm air from the surrounding forest would con-
dense on the little clearing and by the following morning perhaps
the equivalent of a quarter of an inch of rain would have moistened
the patch. No doubt the planners in Whitehall had estimated their
returns on the crops of the Nigerian farmers grown with the help

of the trees. When they bulldozed the forest they wrecked the delicate mechanism by which Nature worked her miracle of growth. The scheme was not only disastrous economically and agriculturally but socially produced repercussions from which Africa might never recover.

Up to the time of the introduction of the ground-nut scheme the status of African administrators had been guaranteed by scientific or political educational training. Settlers had often invested their all in the land they had occupied. Missionaries, too, had been through a rigourous course of training and had felt a vocation before devoting their lives to work in Equatorial Africa. With the bulldozers came a new type of invader—tough, hard, liquor-drinking, often irresponsible artisans with little or no understanding of the country or its peoples. They were highly paid, and their money was easily won and easily spent in drink and gambling. Naturally their example was most injurious to the indigenous people. Moreover, in a few weeks their jobs were being done by Africans who received a small fraction of the payment for the same work. The elders and chiefs had warned the promoters of the danger of removing the essential tree cover. Their advice was disregarded and the experience of men of high standing in forestry and agriculture was not sought.

It was indeed an expensive experiment, involving not only loss of money but the loss of the prestige established by British administrators for a whole century. Instead of reclaiming desert land the scheme had created a new desert, affecting a countryside two hundred miles in length and perhaps one hundred miles wide. It would take many years of adjustment to repair the damage done.

There had been other fields of exploitation in the countries of Africa by the old Colonial powers. In Kenya, American methods of farming with high-speed tractors and chemical fertilizers had created a series of little dustbowls. In Uganda, cotton growing had been responsible for the devastation of much forest country. Similarly in other countries along the Equator, such as French West Africa and the region north of Chad, the desert was allowed to advance.

It became my responsibility to try and stem the destruction in the emerging countries and encourage them to reclaim their deserts.

This work necessitated several journeys to the Sahara to observe the progress of the various large-scale planting projects.

It was after one of these valuable journeys, in 1957, that I returned to England full of constructive ideas, to find the country hell-bent on destruction: hydrogen bombs were being exploded on Christmas Island. This seemed to me utterly opposed to the goodwill that I had been trying to build up through reclaiming the deserts. Surely the time had come to turn from a destructive to a creative way of living? I felt sure that if the people of England appealed to their Sovereign she might intervene with her Ministers to halt these infernal experiments threatening the lives of so many millions. So I started a petition and obtained the signatures of over eight thousand responsible people and members of the Men of the Trees. Accompanied by the Secretary I delivered this petition to the Private Secretary at St. James's Palace and Her Majesty, Queen Elizabeth II, sent it on to the Foreign Office. We were assured by return that the bomb tests would cease. A few days later, however, another bomb was exploded on Christmas Island. All my weeks of work and the goodwill that I had enlisted seemed to be shattered with that bomb. I felt I had to appeal to my friends representing the countries who had assured me of their interest in Sahara Reclamation.

Three days later I was to meet the Ambassadors and Members of the Corps Diplomatique at the twelfth World Forestry Charter Gathering. However, I returned to The Firs, West End, and was sent to bed, as I was running a high temperature. My doctor did what he could, but the temperature refused to respond to treatment but I went to London all the same, desperately hoping that I would be able to influence these diplomats in the cause of peace through the great task of reclaiming the deserts of the world. As usual, I had booked the Park Suite at the Dorchester, Park Lane. As the diplomats arrived I was forced to receive them from a reclining position, though I managed to drag myself to the table as soon as they were all seated. It was a memorable gathering with a record attendance. Many assured me that this was the one event of the year to which they looked forward with keen anticipation. It was a diplomatic occasion of a different sort. All were unanimously agreed in the cause for which I stood. They were all co-partners in a plan which could bring understanding and peace to a confused world. As my old friend, MacDonald, wrote in my Sahara book:

"His plan to reclaim the Sahara is of particular importance. No more imaginative or invaluable piece of constructive work has ever been conceived; and I believe it can also be realized if all governments and other authorities concerned will co-operate in this historic alliance of Man and Nature to make the most famous wilderness in earth bloom like a rose again. That will bring countless blessing to the whole human race."

In a twelve-minute address I summed up the achievements of the past year in country after country. Then ambassador after ambassador rose to assure me that his country would back our Sahara Reclamation Programme. The goodwill that had been generated and the affectionate regard of all those present buoyed me up and enabled me to stand and wish each one goodbye. This was no formal leave-taking; one after another embraced me with gratitude and good wishes for my speedy recovery. By the time the last had left I was exhausted and taken back to my club, where Vincent my valet, helped me to bed. The club doctor came and had me moved to a nursing home in Chelsea. After a restless night, I was moved to the Westminster Hospital where for five days my life hung in the balance. Cables were sent to Shogi Effendi, who for years had been my strong supporter in the work of the Men of the Trees and in my work of Sahara Reclamation. He cabled back to say that he was praying for my recovery at the Holy Shrine on Mount Carmel.

As one medical student after another took samples of my blood, which was of special interest to them as I was a lifelong vegetarian and thus a curiosity in this famous hospital, I felt myself becoming progressively weaker. A visiting friendly doctor who knew what was happening spoke to the physician in charge and I was spared further blood-letting. While still running a high temperature I was allowed to leave hospital after having signed a document absolving the hospital of any responsibility in the event of my death.

Douglas and Aileen Thompson, two very old friends, rescued me and drove me slowly to their home near Winchester where, with the help of Hanworth Walker, then Secretary of the International Vegetarian Union, they nursed me back to convalescence.

It was a long and tedious time. Each evening my temperature rose and over a month passed before it dropped, suddenly, to sub-normal. Gradually in the course of another fortnight it became normal.

While still convalescing I had a visit from my friends from Mount Cook, New Zealand, Catriona Burnett and her aunt, Mrs. Little, who were on their way to the Edinburgh Festival. They invited me to New Zealand, suggesting that the mountain air would revive me. Although I had travelled widely in New Zealand I had never had the opportunity of visiting Mount Cook Station in South Canterbury. The Burnett family had been keen supporters of the Men of the Trees on my previous visit, when I had formed a branch in Central Otago and advised the farmers on tree-planting.

This was the same year as the fifteenth World Vegetarian Union Congress in India to which I had a pressing invitation from the President, Mrs Clarence Gasque, who had been so generous in my battle to save the redwoods, and who now wanted my support in this important Congress. It was decided that I should set out on a cargo boat to Karachi to ensure a peaceful voyage and the full benefit of the sea air.

There were very few other passengers, apart from Pakistani students returning to their country. Going through the Suez Canal I was impressed by the new planting that had taken place since Colonel Nasser had come to power. I took the opportunity of sending him my book, *Land of Tané*, recently off the press, with my congratulations on his planting and a request for an auto-graphed portrait that I might use in the Journal, *Trees*. This duly followed me to New Zealand. It was the first time that the ship's Captain had been through the Canal under the new régime and he remarked that he had been passing through the Canal for thirty-two years and had never experienced less delay.

My health gradually improved and on arrival at Karachi I pre-sented one of my walking-sticks to the Captain as a thank you and souvenir of the voyage which had done me so much good. At the gangway I was met by three Bahá'ís who sadly reported that my dear friend, Shogi Effendi had fallen critically ill in London with Asian 'flu. The local Bahá'í Committee had decided to hold a prayer meeting which they asked me to conduct and I readily agreed to this.

The following night I was due to lecture on the Sahara and show a film for the British Council. They had very kindly put me up at the Palace Hotel where I was able to receive delegates to an F.A.O. Symposium on Arid Zones. A large contingent of the delegates came to my lecture and the following night I was invited to attend a reception to meet the delegates from Rome and the Near East. It had long been my desire to meet the authorities on Arid Zones and Desert Reclamation, but I had not realized that my arrival in Karachi would coincide with this Symposium. In fact, since I was first introduced to the Bahá'í faith it has been my experience that whenever I have put their cause first, my work for the Men of the Trees and land reclamation has prospered enormously.

In spite of my severe illness and slow recovery, I was able to advise the Ministry of Agriculture on the Reclamation of the Sind Desert before going on to Bombay, for the Fifteenth World Vegetarian Union Congress. When I got to my hotel a deputation of five distressed Bahá'ís of the Bombay Community were waiting at the door to tell me the sad news of the passing of the beloved Guardian. They said they were going to have an all-night prayer meeting and asked me to conduct it. Although I was exhausted from the journey and still suffering from the after-effects of my illness I felt I could not do other than consent.

Taking leave of my fellow delegates I accompanied my Bahá'í friends to their headquarters. It was an upstairs room, filled to overflowing; even the stairway was crowded. I find it difficult to convey the severe shock experienced by the Bombay believers among whom there was a sense of personal bereavement. Indeed, they all seemed stricken, sobbing as though their hearts were completely broken. It was to the prayers of Bahá'u'lláh and Abdul Bahá that I turned for comfort and inspiration and soon these were being chanted by Persians and Indians in their own languages. Frequently through the night we returned to the Tablet of Ahmed which I recited in English, to be followed in Persian and the languages of all those present. Dawn was breaking when I brought the meeting to a close and returned to my hotel to snatch a couple of hour's rest before breakfast and a full programme arranged for the delegates.

I was invited to take part in the first Symposium and thereafter was constantly called upon by the President to propose votes of thanks to our hospitable hosts who had arranged luncheons and dinners to meet Indian friends and members of the Bombay Humanitarian League.

Despite the extraordinary physical and mental exertion, I found myself daily getting stronger. Far from taxing my strength, the all-night prayer meeting had proved an exhilarating experience which I shall never forget. The affection of the Bahá'í friends, with whom it had been my privilege to share their sorrow, buoyed me up and prepared me for the arduous time before me.

Travelling to New Delhi in the train, glad of a few quiet moments, I sat by myself in the corner of the carriage, looking out on the poor little farms and the sad, dry countryside. Later, Dan Hoffman who had met me for the first time on this train reminded me of this journey. Years afterwards he told me that he had first seen me gazing out on this sandy waste. My first words to him were, "Oh, if only they had a few trees!".

In the midst of a very full conference programme in New Delhi I was taken to see Prime Minister Nehru by Rukmini Devi Arundale, a member of Parliament and one of the principal hostesses to the Conference.

"Baker, I have read your book, *Sahara Challenge*, three times," were Nehru's first words. Now what are we going to do about the Indian deserts?"

"The answer is the same," I said. "Trees against the desert."

"But," he exclaimed, "the desert's only a hundred miles away and whenever the wind is blowing in this direction the visibility becomes poor and the windows have to be closed to keep out the dust."

"The fields must be tree-surrounded and reduced in size. Trees are needed to fix the soil and lift the spring water table and keep the land cool," I said.

We talked on these lines for some time and then he asked me if I would be prepared to meet the Minister of Agriculture and the Forestry people. He pressed a button on his desk and the Minister of Agriculture appeared.

"I want you two to get together," said Nehru.

I agreed to meet the Minister for a conference the next morning at ten o'clock.

From then on I had to forego the Congress for about ten days. I was invited to Dehra Dun to lecture to the professors and teaching staff of the forestry school and to spend two days with the students and research departments. It was not until the Congress had reached Madras that I was able to catch up with it.

The sequel to the advice I had given was that after five years food was increased by fifteen per cent, and after ten years by thirty per cent. Eleven years later when I revisited India, I learned that similar planting programmes of shelter belts and shade trees have helped to increase food production up to a hundred per cent.

From New Delhi I went by train to Madras, where I was entertained at lunch by the Maharajah of Baroda, who told me that his favourite book was *Green Glory, Forests of the World,* though he had also read many of my other books. I continued my journey to Colombo, Ceylon, where I had the opportunity of seeing the progress made in the Chena Plantations which had resulted from my previous visit in 1931. I was warmly greeted by the Chief Conservator of Forests, who proudly showed me his Forest Institute and forestry working plans. In Colombo I also met the publisher of *Green Glory* in Singhalese, which had a foreward by the Ceylon High Commissioner in London.

On the day I was due to leave for Sydney on the *Himalaya* there was a general strike in Colombo. The ship had to anchor off-shore and launch a lifeboat to take the passengers on board. I reached the ship with great relief and found that a comfortable cabin had been reserved for me by my friends at Mount Cook. After I had given three lectures and shown my Sahara films, the only way I could get some quiet was to accept the Captain's kind invitation to make use of his sitting-room.

The voyage passed all too quickly. On my arrival in Sydney I was greeted by the Men of the Land. This Society had started as Men of the Trees but after some years it was decided to change the name to enlist the interest of farmers.

Sydney was very hot and I was glad to get on board the Auckland boat. The weather was rough but by this time I had got my sea legs. I arrived at Auckland with keen expectation, only to find a message from Mount Cook Station asking me to postpone my visit for a while and suggesting I should take the opportunity of seeing my old friend, Sam Williams of Mangakuri. As there was time to spare I decided to visit Spirits Bay, in the extreme north of the North Island to become acquainted with the Pohutukawa tree by which the spirits of Maoris leave this life and proceed to the Underworld. As I descended the steep hillside towards the Bay, my knees seemed to be giving way and for a while I wondered if I would ever get back. My spirit seemed to be joining the generations of Maoris who had passed that way to the Underworld by the lonely Pohutukawa tree.

Now it was Christmas 1957 and I was happy to be seeing my old friend once again. He and his elder brother had joined up for Christmas and it was a real family reunion. Sam's niece, Patricia, back from Woodford House at Havelock North, had brought with her half-a-dozen Rarotonga girls who were working at the school. They put on native costume and did hula-hula dances for entertainment.

Eventually I got to Mount Cook, which had been marooned when the road was cut by the river and had only just recently been opened again.

After a very pleasant stay at Mount Cook, when I had moved on to visit other friends, I began to realize that something was missing. It soon dawned on me that I had become accustomed to the life at Mount Cook and had become fond of Catriona. So I sat down and wrote, asking her to marry me. In the letter I said I would ring up at ten o'clock on Monday morning to get her decision. It was a long-distance call and the last thirty miles was single line. At the time there was a furious storm raging, which was causing considerable interference on the line; it was as much as I could do to hear her shouting back, "Yes, Yes!" It seemed strange to her that although there had been plenty of opportunities for proposing under idyllic conditions a Man of the Trees should wait until he had gone away and then expect to get an answer on a bad line in the middle of a storm!

Although at Mount Cook I had hankered for a ride for a long time, it was not until the last day that I was able to help move a mob of fifteen hundred sheep over the hills to fresh pastures. That

day I was in the saddle for eleven hours and after this experience I
felt I was qualified to undertake the "Cobbett Ride" which I did
on my return to England.

As a boy I had heard so much about William Cobbett, who had
lived at Steeple Court, Botley, when my great-grandfather was
Rector. At Botley Cobbett had his nurseries when he brought
acacia seed back from Tennessee and Long Island. He had written
at length about the virtues of what he called the "locust tree"; it
was *robinia pseudo acacia*, named after M. Robin, the famous
French botanist. Cobbett had prophesied that this acacia would
take the place of oak for the wooden walls of England. Little did
he think in those days that steel would take the place of both. The
old housekeeper from the Rectory used to tell my father that,
throughout the planting season, bundles of Cobbett acacia were
taken by coaches to all parts of England. It became a patriotic thing
to plant Cobbett's acacia. It was excellent for making ships' wooden
nails. A gatepost of it would stand in the ground for one hundred
years while oak would last about forty-five. Besides, it was a soil
improver; being leguminous, it impregnated the ground with
nitrogen. However, its popularity did not last very long because
gamekeepers did not like the thorns, and for many decades tree-
planting became subservient to shooting. Cobbett had borrowed
money in Botley and when he returned from America, apparently
prosperous, the old Rector suggested to him that it might be
helpful if he repaid his debts. One woman had been widowed and
the Rector felt that she needed the money she had lent him.
Cobbett strongly resented the interference of the Rector in what
he considered his private affairs, and ever after that he would ride
a long way round to avoid meeting parson Baker!

When the Society of Journalists decided to put up a memorial
to Cobbett at Botley, it occurred to me that it would be a good
opportunity to follow in his hoofprints, putting two of his rural
rides together, covering about three hundred and thirty miles
through Hampshire, Surrey and Sussex, returning in time for the
unveiling of the memorial. Owing to my illness this had had to be
postponed, but now, having returned to England I undertook this,
lecturing to about five schools a day on William Cobbett and tree-
planting. On completing the journey at Botley I gave a luncheon

to as many of his descendants as I could muster. I invited the Mayor of Southampton to be present to help me to mark this occasion. Also present were Members of the Council of the Men of the Trees, and Gerald Fergusson, President of the Men of the Trees in New Zealand, and his wife. It was an historic occasion and I trust that the Baker ghost was well and truly laid!

For my children's holidays I had arranged for them to go on a riding tour beginning from Alton in Hampshire. I started them off in the morning and, having arranged to meet them on the other side of Winchester, twenty-five miles away, found myself free for the day. I decided to join the Surrey Gliding Club at Lasham and take some lessons. The only time I had ever won a first prize for essay-writing was at college when I wrote one on flying! Blériot had just crossed the Channel for the first time, and in my essay I quoted someone who had described his first experience of flying as "smoother and softer than dreaming". I soon realised how much more this applied to gliding. It was a wonderful experience to be able to glide over forestry plantations and woodlands. On a hot day one got a good thermal lift over forest areas and could glide from forest to forest.

After some days of enjoyment it seemed hardly fair for me to expect an airman to tow me up to four thousand feet without repaying the compliment. It was usual for members to take turns, for the majority of them were air pilots, so I joined the Hampshire Aero Club and became a student pilot myself. At the end of my first lesson which lasted three-quarters of an hour, the President of the Club, Captain Bellamy, a flying ace who owned his private Spitfire, met me as I was walking in from the Hornet I had been flying and said: "Baker, are you flying solo yet?" I was somewhat taken aback but managed to retort: "Not yet, I am waiting till I can borrow your Spitfire!" "Right, Hawkins " he said to my instructor, "remember that when he's flying solo I insist on him flying my Spitfire!"

In the course of my lessons I was given special dispensation from the Control Tower to fly above the country which I had ridden over on horseback in the hoofprints of William Cobbett. I covered what had taken me three weeks on horseback in just over three hours in the air.

Chapter 10

A NEW LIFE IN THE ANTIPODES

My road calls me, lures me
East, West, South and North;
Most roads lead men homewards,
My road leads me forth.

To add more miles to the tally
Of grey miles left behind,
In quest of that one beauty
God put me here to find.

(By kind permission of John Masefield
and Publishers)'

I HAD BEEN WAITING for a cancellation on the *Rangitani* to travel to New Zealand. This did not materialize, but I persuaded the purser to take my hand baggage. I had already forwarded my personal effects including thirteen cases of my library books; already half my library had been given to the Men of the Trees, and before that a third to the Forestry School in Palestine.

Having seen my baggage safely stowed on board, I decided to fly. On my way back from the docks, I was strolling along Piccadilly and, passing Sabena Airways, I went in to inquire if they had a flight to New Zealand. Looking at the sparkling lights dotted across the world on the wall of the offices, I came to the conclusion that the shortest way to Auckland was through Moscow, and asked if there was any chance of returning that way.

"Have you got a visa for the U.S.S.R.?" inquired the manager.

I admitted I had not. He gave me an address near the B.B.C. When I arrived there the Russian asked: "Have you got a ticket?" and gave me an address in the neighbourhood where I could obtain one. He said the travel agents would arrange for a visa and ration ticket. A few minutes later I was in the agent's office, asking whether it would be possible to get a seat on the latest Russian jet which we had been hearing so much about. The girl behind the

desk said she would inquire and, after telephoning said she had
reserved a place on the latest jet, leaving the following day at one
o'clock. If I gave her my passport and ten pounds on account she
would do the rest; and I could call at ten o'clock the following
morning to collect my ticket.

As soon as I had boarded the plane I gave my card to the air
hostess, and said:

"As a student pilot I'd very much like to go forward and see the
works."

A message soon came back to the effect that I would be called
forward as soon as we had 'hit the ceiling'. Ten minutes later I was
sent for by the Captain. I told him the story of my first flying
lesson and Bellamy's invitation to fly his Spitfire which I had been
unable to take up because of rough weather. I said I should very
much like to fly his jet instead so that I could tell Bellamy So I
was allowed to fly the fastest jet in the world on Bellamy's reputation! As soon as I had got the feel of it I handed the controls
back to the Captain and, after inspecting the complicated set-up
and speaking to most of the officers, returned to my seat. Hugh
Gaitskell, then Leader of the Opposition, and Aneurin Bevan were
also on the plane and made pleasant travelling companions.

The distinguished Labour Leaders were given a big welcome at
Moscow Airport. The following day, however, I was given a royal
welcome by the plant pathologists, botanists and ecologists, as
well as the agricultural and forestry people. *Green Glory—Forests
of the World* had become a textbook and was being used by
Government Departments. A summary had been circulated among
the schools of the country. Excitement was running high over the
recent discovery or adaptation of a tree that would survive under
desert conditions with a minimum amount of moisture. For ten
years nurserymen and plant breeders in Hungary, Poland and the
U.S.S.R. had combined in research to produce this tree which
looked rather like a poplar. At the time of my visit it had not been
named botanically but it was known as the Peace Tree. The warm
welcome I received was quite unexpected and I was overwhelmed
by the generous appreciation of my books and my work in desert
reclamation.

On Sunday evening I strolled along a boulevard by the Kremlin with Billy Graham's righthand man, who told me he had attended three full services at the Methodist Church where they had six thousand subscribing members. At each service there had been two thousand people. This gave the lie to the reports in the Western Press about the irreligious people of the U.S.S.R.

The American exhibition was on in Moscow and excursions from Chicago and New York were bringing thousands of Americans to the city to see their own exhibition now being thronged by tens of thousands of Russians. This exhibition was regarded as a show by the Russian people who were intrigued by the fashion parades, such as the correct clothes for a schoolgirl at different hours of the day and for work or play. Her first cocktail party dress drew an admiring crowd of Muscovites to whom it was most revealing that children should be dressed up to drink! They were bewildered by the many changes of costume for the various kinds of sport, social and college activities. At that time the average Russian would have his best suit and his not-so-best and his working clothes; the same would apply to women. They gazed in admiration at the thousand-and-one changes and gadgets of the West which they could not imagine necessary, nor were they tempted to buy. After eight and a half days, far too short a time, I left for India to see what progress was being made with the shelter belts I had helped Nehru to inaugurate.

I was ahead of time when I arrived in New Zealand and so was able to return once again to the Kauri forests and visit the forestry research people before going to Timaru. The little town was astir in anticipation of the wedding of the daughter of its most illustrious citizen and benefactor of St. David's, the little church built by the father of the bride in memory of the early runholders (or sheep-farmers). It was the first time a member of the Burnett family was to be married there. The bride was coming from Mount Cook Station, a hundred miles away, and the bridegroom more than twelve thousand miles, from his old family home in the South of England which he had sacrificed for the lady of his choice. Only a hundred of the four hundred guests could fit into the church; however, all gathered in the large marquee on the lawn of the Burnett family's house at Cave for the wedding breakfast. The wedding cake was surmounted by a living Western Red Cedar

to be planted afterwards hard by the Sunday School, which was
built by the bride in memory of her mother.

Just as we drove off after the wedding breakfast, having got
clear of the confetti-throwers, Catriona leaned towards me and
said:

"Richard, my wedding present to you is a horse".

"Darling," I said, "you couldn't have thought of anything
better."

We were to spend our honeymoon on Stewart Island with its
unspoilt indigenous forest but had only reached Dunedin by the
first night and Invercargill by the second. The much-looked-forward-
to honeymoon melted into a flight to the Island, a taxi drive
along the beaches to various look-out places and back by stages to
Mount Cook, where the bride was indispensable during mustering
and shearing.

Carpenters were busy enlarging the homestead, building extra
rooms and bathroom for the additional family and I got their help
in putting up shelves in my study den. There were my thirteen
cases of books to be housed, besides files, records, manuscripts
and stationery. It was understood that I should provide headquarters for the Dominion and Overseas Members of the Men of
the Trees. This part of our work had become increasingly more
important ever since the First Sahara University Expedition.

Catriona had the idea of postponing the honeymoon until my
children, Angela and Paul, came out for their next holiday at the
height of the ski-ing season. It was good to see Angela making use
of the ski lift and ski-ing confidently at speed, while Paul was
having his first lessons from an Austrian professional. Later we
enjoyed skating at Lake Tekapo before setting out for the First
Redwood Reunion in California.

While I was attending the Fifth World Forestry Congress in
Seattle, Catriona and the children were the guests of my old
friends John and Ethel de Blois Wack at Santa Barbara. We all
joined the Men of the Trees from England at the Plaza Hotel, San
Francisco and set out the following day along the Redwood
Empire Highway to Eureka. We approached Mill Creek from the
Coast where the road wound its way through redwood trees three
hundred feet high and turned off into a glade in the heart of the

Grove of Understanding for the reunion.

This reunion was a very happy time for me. In contrast I was torn at having to say good-bye to Angela and Paul as I saw them off on their plane to England. I had to return to New Zealand to settle down to the routine of station life.

I soon found that I had to rise at four to cope with my writing, as this gave me four uninterrupted hours before breakfast, after which I threw myself into the day's work on the station. When I was not needed to help with the animals I devoted myself to the garden, where I erected three bins to provide organic compost for the vegetables which were my special care. My wife and her brother had given me a kit-set greenhouse as a birthday present. I erected this with a boy's help and was able to raise all sorts of vegetables— tomatoes, lettuce and mustard and cress.

Just as I was beginning to wonder if my promised wedding present would materialize, Catriona said she had bought me a fine chestnut cob, which belonged to a farmer at Aubury. She had heard from the farmer that the mare was somewhat of an unknown character, but as he had been able to shoe her, Catriona thought her husband would be able to ride her! As the mare was not used to going in a horse-box, Catriona said she would drive me over the next morning and I could ride back—it was only eighty miles away!

I was too trusting when tightening the girth and this fine-looking horse nipped my seat! Not a good beginning! Eventually I rode her home, spending one night in the hotel at Burkes Pass. Passing through Lake Tekapo schoolboys asked me what had happened to her tail? The poor thing had been docked—a brutal practice, fortunately now out of fashion. It is trying for a horse not to have a long tail in fly country, particularly in summertime. This mare, Tui, however could kick a fly's eye out! After some years of faithful service I lent her to a cousin of Catriona's as I was going back to the Sahara. When I returned to Mount Cook, Tui had met with a serious accident, having become entangled in a barbed wire fence, and had had to be put down. Catriona greeted me with a new horse, to replace her, a beautiful palomino with long silver mane and tail whom I christened Saha, Arabic for "good health". He is a rough ride but good on the hills and can pack a load—a friendly creature who surprises guests by walking into the cookhouse.

In June 1963 a young Dutchman had decided to ride through New Zealand on horseback. He started out with a riding horse and two pack horses. Unfortunately, one of the horses was struck by a motor-bike coming round a bend at 70 m.p.h. A second stood on a soft shoulder of the Coromandel Peninsula and fell a thousand feet to its death, and the third was killed by an articulated lorry travelling at speed. So the poor fellow lost his horses, his bet and the chance of making a record ride. This seemed to offer a challenge to me and I decided to make an attempt to ride one horse, carrying my sleeping bag, haversack, and oats on the saddle.

Before starting out on this adventure, I wrote to my old friend and publisher, A.H. Reed, who had walked the length of the Islands, and told him I thought that as he had managed to walk twelve hundred miles I hoped that I would be able to ride from the most northerly kauri to the most southerly. I was intending to start at the Waipoa Forest. He replied that that would be cheating because the most northerly kauri was situated near the lighthouse on the farm of Mr. Keen, the most northerly farmer in New Zealand. Mr. Reed advised me to invite myself for a night on Keen's farm; he would be able to direct me to the young kauris at the northernmost point of North Island. I followed this suggestion, taking my saddle with me.

I borrowed various horses, always searching for the perfect horse for the job, but it was not until I reached Kaikohe that I acquired Rajah, an aged dark bay and a famous jumper. At the time I acquired him I did not realise he was unaccustomed to journeys and that he had always travelled from show to show by horse-box. In fact, years afterwards, I heard that the father of the owner had bet his son five pounds I would not get more than twenty miles down the road. The first day I did thirty-two, ending up in the rain. I had given talks to six schools on the way and Rajah seemed rather tired. So we decided that twenty-five miles and five schools a day would be better.

There had been much publicity when the young Dutchman set out on his marathon ride, but I decided I would say nothing about my effort to the Press, until there was some likelihood of my being able to achieve it. One morning, however, on the outskirts of Auckland, I was saddling up in the rain when a television cameraman arrived and followed our movements until I had mounted and set off. That evening Rajah and the ride ceased to be a secret and wherever we went throughout the North Island there was keen expectation at the schools. We might do twenty miles before breakfast and turn up at the main school of a town as the pupils were arriving. I would ask if there were any members of the pony clubs present—maybe four of the children would hold up their hands, whereupon I would hand over Rajah to two of them and ask the other two to stand near his hind-quarters to keep the other children away. While I was talking to the principal the children would crowd to stroke the horse and when the pressure became strong, Rajah would lift his head and send them flying head over heels. Amid much merriment they would rally again and once more he would repeat the trick. He was always a great favourite with the children and very gentle.

Towards four o'clock in the afternoon, Rajah would indicate that he had had enough, especially if there was a strong head wind. He would lower his head as if to say: "What about it?"

He was a wonderful partner and I let him choose his pace and distance. Towards the end of the ride a reporter from the *Southland Times* came out to meet us and after interviewing me, said, "Excuse me, sir, but would you mind telling me your age?"

To which I replied, "If you guess Rajah's age precisely, I will tell you mine."

He looked at Rajah's glossy coat and said, "Six, sir?"

I shook my head, and said, "Nearer sixteen."

I did not tell him my age. It did not seem important or part of the story; besides when you have a young wife and two children it is not funny to be headlines in the national Press: "Seventy-four-year-old Dominion rider nearing the end of his journey"!

The deputy Mayor of Invercargill, the most southerly city, was waiting to greet me as I rode up to what I thought was the most southerly kauri in the southern hemisphere. Alan Calvert, honorary secretary of the Men of the Trees for Southland, had selected an excellent home for Rajah as I had decided it would not be fair to take him to our inhospitable tussock country at Mount Cook, so I presented him to Flora Johnstone, daughter of the President elect of the Men of the Trees. Rajah was put into the same paddock as

Flora's other horse, Sultan, and soon became close friends with him and Flora.

After the ride I visited Stewart Island, where I found three more Kauri trees, one of which must have been the most southerly kauri of all. On my return from Stewart Island I spent three memorable days walking on the Milford Track, often described as the most beautiful walk in the world. For years this had been a dream of mine, but pressure of work and the thought that I was not justified in spending the money had made me postpone this. Now at last through the kind thought of a Southland member of the Men of the Trees it was made possible. After my twelve-hundred-mile ride and the daily exercise of grooming Rajah I was unlikely ever to be fitter. I was fortunate enough to have as my guide Bill Anderson who with his own hands had built many miles of the trail, zigzagging up the mountain sides to make climbing easier for the amateur climber or placing stepping-stones in mountain torrents.

Five years later, just before my 1968 Expedition, I revisited Southland and had a delightful reunion with Flora, Rajah and Sultan. Rajah came to my call, walking sedately across the paddock to the gate where I stood with a double handful of crushed oats. He did not look a day older than when I had given him to Flora at the end of my ride. He was still winning gymkhana prizes for Flora who had developed into a beautiful young woman at nineteen and was worshipped by the young men of Southland. Month by month Flora used to report on her progress with Rajah in show-ring or paddock. How fortunate Rajah had been in this acquaintance which had ripened into understanding friendship!

That night my mind went back over the ride from its first inception. It had all started with a confession I had made in a letter to the Chairman of the National Spiritual Assembly of the Bahá'ís of New Zealand. At the time I was beginning to feel that I was living a selfish life, enjoying superb mountain scenery and all the comfort of a perfectly run home at Mount Cook, without being of much use to my fellow-men and women. True, I had kept in touch with Africa and my Sahara Reclamation Programme and had managed to interest one hundred and eight countries in this work of regeneration by tree-planting, and many billions of trees were well and truly planted and growing. I realised that there had to be periods of rest and refreshment in between intensive endeavour. But I knew in my heart that the time had come to launch out once more into the world of humanity.

A Baha'i friend was Chairman of the United Nations Association and his Committee suggested that I be invited to give a series of lectures in connection with their Freedom from Hunger Year. It was easy to see how my Sahara Reclamation Programme fitted in with this and how my Sahara films and slides could be turned to good account. My first lecture was to be on a Sunday afternoon in the Winter Gardens at Hamilton, a month later another one at Auckland, and others in various towns through the Islands as far south as Invercargill. Here was a god-given opportunity to serve my fellow-men; so in consultation with Catriona I accepted the invitation and set out with my saddle and nose-bag. When not lecturing directly for the United Nations Association I could talk to the boys and girls of New Zealand on the importance of handing on our tree heritage. As my mind went back over the ninety-two thousand or so young New Zealanders whom I had met during my ride, I found myself wondering how many of them would be devoting their lives to the service of their fellow-men in handing on our tree heritage for others to enjoy. Their road may in the end call them to become leaders in the Army of the Green Front.

Chapter 11

25,000 MILES AROUND THE SAHARA

The wilderness and the solitary place shall be glad . . .
the desert shall rejoice and blossom as the rose.

Isaiah 35:1

SOON AFTER MY RETURN to Mount Cook from my Dominion ride, a cable came from the President of the Conservation Committee of California inviting me to attend a special meeting called to help to avert a new threat to the redwoods. A new six-lane freeway was to be cut through the heart of the groves, including the twelve thousand acres of redwoods I had fought for so hard and for so long, which had been handed over to the State of California in 1939 "to be preserved for all time". An alternative route was proposed, but was unacceptable to the lumbermen as it entailed hauling up and down hill and would therefore use more petrol.

It looked as if some of the most beautiful of the remaining stands of redwoods, including the Grove of Understanding, were to be sacrificed to speed. The Geographical Society had offered a prize of eighty thousand dollars to anybody who would draw up an acceptable route along the coast, which would cause as little destruction as possible.

It was in desperation therefore that the Californian Conservationists cabled me. Three days later I was in conference with them in Santa Barbara. There I was deputed to see the Chairman of the Natural Resources in Canada, Mr Charles de Turk, in Sacramento. He introduced me to the heads of his various Departments of Parks and Beaches and together we studied an alternative route upon which they agreed. As the Federal Government was paying ninety-five per cent of the cost of the construction of the new freeway, the Chairman suggested that I should visit Secretary Udall of the Department of the Interior at Washington, which I agreed to do.

A few days later I was in Washington, where I was met by Major-General Pletcher, who had served on the Council of the Men of the Trees when he was acting as military attaché for his Government in Southampton. An audience was arranged with Secretary Udall, who had just returned from West Germany and, in spite of there being a long line of people waiting to see him, he was good enough to see me first. I was with him for about twenty minutes and he agreed to the alternative route which I suggested, but said, "We must keep our fingers crossed, as this will have to go before Congress and many committees."

The country was now aroused to the importance of creating a National Redwood Park. The Sierra Club claimed that the area should not be twenty thousand acres, but two hundred thousand acres and indicated the area they had in mind. Thereupon lumber companies waded in and felled some of the choicest groves with the object of killing the project, and although the Government placed an injunction upon them to prohibit further felling while the question of a National Redwood Park was under consideration, the damage had already been done. Another party of conservationists had set their heart on preserving an area in which they claimed was the tallest tree in the world. With this rivalry of conservationists there was a risk of losing out to the lumbermen and sacrificing what had already been acquired through our long years of endeavour.

The struggle to save the redwoods still goes on; it seems that each generation will have to fight to maintain their redwood heritage.

In New York I went on the air again with Lowell Thomas in *World News* and spoke both of the new threat to the redwoods and of the importance of desert reclamation, including the dustbowl of the U.S.A. I strongly advocated the establishment of five more shelter belts from the Canadian border down to the Panhandle of Texas to arrest erosion and desiccation and make it possible to accommodate the growing population in that great country.

Before leaving California, however, with the help of Dr. Knut Scharnhorst, General Secretary of the Sahara Reclamation Programme, I drafted and dispatched individual letters to Heads of State in the countries in and around the Sahara, inviting them to a conference in Rabat.

Back in London I recruited members of the Men of the Trees to form a party to join the Rabat Conference. The B.B.C. arranged to make a film on desert reclamation in Morocco and their cameramen and producer met us on the fringe of the Sahara in South Morocco a few days after the Conference. A vast project known as the Sahara Reclamation Programme was launched. Cables supporting the idea were received from Heads of State and I set out on my twenty-five-thousand-mile journey around the Sahara to visit them in their own territories. The story of this is briefly recorded in *Sahara Conquest*, a sequel to *Sahara Challenge*.

Since my first Sahara University Expedition a new Africa had emerged. Instead of the continent being exploited by five colonial powers, twenty-five countries had come into being and these countries were now preparing to unite in reclaiming the Sahara. If two million square miles of the world's most famous desert could be made to grow food, it would be virtually adding a new continent to the world. The Sixth World Forestry Congress which opened in Madrid on June 6, 1966, gave me an opportunity to represent the twenty-four countries I had visited in and around the Sahara and the delegates from those countries were my guests at the Hogar Restaurant. This enabled them to come together for the first time and meet each other socially and overcome old prejudices.

The Sahara Reclamation Programme provides a challenge so arresting that it could unite all the countries who have fought so long for their freedom and liberation from colonialism.

In October 1966 I was invited by Henry B. Stevens of New Hampshire to a vegetarian lunch in London, when I was presented with the Millenium Guild of New York Freshel Award of one thousand dollars for *Sahara Conquest*. This is an award presented annually to the writer of the book making the greatest contribution to humanitarianism. On my return to New Zealand I was pleasantly surprised to be welcomed by the Lord Mayor of Wellington, the British High Commissioner, the Canadian Trade Commissioner, and a number of professors from the University. It was the first time this particular award had come to New Zealand and this was their way of honouring me. Later a television interview in the Park followed and I had a reunion with my Publishers, A.H. and A.W. Reed, who had produced *Famous Trees of New Zealand*.

I was particularly pleased that my daughter Angela was able to obtain special leave to come and meet my boat. At the time she was taking the Community Nursing Course at Nelson, having already taken her university entrance examination.

At Mount Cook I found a mountain of mail to greet me. I used to have a theory that if one left mail unanswered long enough it would answer itself, but I have long since found this to be a fallacy!

I had a growing feeling that it was imperative to step up the planting programme in New Zealand because for every single substitute for wood in the world today there are about ten new uses for forest products in one form or another. With the spread of education an increasing amount of paper is needed for books and magazines. Fibres and fabrics made from wood are replacing wool.

Forty-two years before my father-in-law had planted half a million trees on Mount Cook Station, and as a forester I found it interesting to work out the wood increment and see how the returns compared with sheep-farming. The returns from the shelter belts and plantations proved to be forty times higher than those from wool. In that country five acres support one sheep which brings a return of ten shillings a year; in other words, the return amounts to only two shillings per acre as compared with four pounds under timber. Inspired by these figures I started out on a forestry fact-finding mission throughout New Zealand to discover how much more land might be devoted to forestry. It was heartening that as a result of my endeavour I was able to persuade the Government to double the planting programme.

Later I set out on a forestry tour of Australia. Journeying through Queensland I was shocked to find miles and miles of eucalyptus forest being felled to make cattle runs. Small farmers were being encouraged to take land newly broken up and sown to grass. With the removal of the forest the water cycle was broken, rain and dew were becoming less and less and desert conditions threatening the country. I managed to give some Press and television interviews which sparked off interest in desert reclamation, before returning to New Zealand.

Sahara Challenge had alerted and created international interest, as well as prompting investments in the natural resources of an emerging continent. *Sahara Conquest* appealed to the individual with humanitarian inclinations and made him wish to throw in his lot on the Green Front against the Desert. Hardly a day passed without my receiving offers of help. Sometimes a professor would write saying that he had read my book with deepening interest and that he and his family had decided to spend the rest of their days in devotion to desert reclamation, if a place could be found for them. Often money was of little concern to them; it was the humanitarian aspect of the venture which attracted them. My colleague, Dr. Knut Scharnhorst, had sold his interests in America with a view to assisting me to establish an Institute for Research in Nutrition and Land Reclamation. He was convinced that a grano-fructarian way of life would be the order of the day among the Sahara peoples and he wished to demonstrate this idea.

Following my twenty-five-thousand-mile journey around the Sahara, I thought I had successfully handed the Sahara Reclamation Programme over to the Heads of State and various organizations responsible for the economic and social welfare of the surrounding Saharan countries. I was therefore shocked by the events of the tragic upheaval in Nigeria and Ghana which had both been so full of promise. In Nigeria I had initiated silvicultural experiments and trained an African staff in practical administration of their forest estates. In Ghana I had rated President Kwame Nkrumah with President Bourguiba as being in the vanguard of the fight for freedom. It seemed as soon as I went back to New Zealand these emerging countries about whom I had been so happy, had had their authority undermined. The old policy of 'divide and rule' was re-employed to disrupt newly acquired unity largely based on Sahara Reclamation.

Thus I felt I had failed in my bid to create unity among the countries of the Sahara, and must once again return to renew the struggle. About the time that I came to this conclusion there were reports that many Indians were losing their work in Kenya and finding it difficult to get employment elsewhere. It occured to me that their services would be invaluable in many of the countries where they could obtain work in desert reclamation. This prompted

me to visit the High Commissioner for India in Wellington and
suggest that there might be openings for his countrymen on the
Green Front against the Desert.

"But," he said, "we have our own desert problems in India, we
want your help there. Already the Indian desert is threatening
New Delhi and the situation is becoming very serious. Would it not
be possible for you to see the situation for yourself and advise my
Government?"

This I consented to do at the very first opportunity, realizing
that having reached India I should be half-way to Africa. I knew
that if I could persuade the present Government of India to tackle
their planting programme and extend the idea of shelter belts and
tree-surrounded fields, food production might be substantially
increased and the encroaching desert held at bay.

Some weeks later, in New Delhi, I was met by the Inspector-
General of Forests, who used my visit to create interest for land
reclamation and increased food production by tree-planting.
I was invited to meet various ministers in the Government, including the Minister of Planning, the Minister for Food and
the deputy Prime Minister, Mr Morarji Desai. After discussing
these problems with the officials I gave a broadcast intended
to create interest for the implementation of the plans which
I had proposed.

The desert question was not only an Indian problem: it belonged
equally to Pakistan, where the Sind desert merged into the Indian
desert. My next mission was therefore to Karachi to enlist the
co-operation of President Ayub Khan, who I gathered was a great
tree-lover and well aware of the biological contribution of trees. I
was heartened to see that some of my planting suggestions of
eleven years previously had been followed with some success. In
contrast to India, Pakistan seemed largely to have solved the
problem of unemployment and feeding their population.

I wondered whether the religious background of Islam was
influencing the material welfare of the people. In Morocco before
the King had launched his successful planting programme for
youth, known as the Forêts Jeunesse, the Muezzin had broadcast
passages from the Koran referring to the rewards in store for the
planters of trees. In Pakistan I was once more reminded of the fact

that every Moslem treats the Koran not only as a guide to Heaven but also as a handbook for daily living.

As I expected to see more of the North African countries in the future, I took the opportunity of learning more about Islam. I wondered if the Holy Men of India, many of whom were too holy to work and had become professional beggers, had influenced some of the communities of India to follow their example, to the great detriment of the country.

Next I visited Kuwait. On my arrival there, I was welcomed by His Excellency Al-Rifai, Cabinet Minister at the Palace, and Badr Al Majid, Private Secretary to His Highness, the Sheikh of Kuwait. His Highness was visiting Lebanon and I was urged to return again as soon as possible. A broadcast interview before I left gave me an opportunity of paying tribute to the fine work of shelter-belt planting under the most trying conditions, and wishing success to their imaginative planting plan to protect Kuwait from the drying winds of the desert by creating a local micro-climate.

In Kuwait, a strictly Moslem country, tree-planting was flourishing and a very extensive shelter-belt programme was being promoted. The desert was being reclaimed with the help of city waste and sewage—not a drop of which was wasted. Despite temperatures rising to over 130° Fahrenheit and practically no rainfall, it was encouraging to find several kinds of acacias flourishing.

What struck me about this country was the absence of poverty and the spontaneous kindness of the people. Under the wise and benevolent leadership of Sheikh Abdullah Al-Salem Al Sabah and the democratic National Assembly Government, Kuwait's "black-gold", as the oil is called, has been wisely used for the advancement and well-being of the people, with the result that Kuwait has become one of the world's most vital and progressive countries.

While in Kuwait I was shocked to hear of the devastating earthquakes in Iran. It occured to me that New Zealand might be able to send over some of the kit-set houses, packed in four ordinary trailer loads, for the survivors of the earthquake. In Bombay I had explored ways and means for supplying some of the million and a half homeless with little wooden houses, each of which could shelter up to ten or twelve and provide a bunk where they could sleep and keep a change of clothes.

It had long been my desire to visit the cedars of Lebanon, and if possible to do something to perpetuate them. For many years I had studied reports and been engaged in research for my book, *Famous Trees of Bible Lands*. Isaiah had written: "The glory of Lebanon shall come to thee . . . and I will make the place of my feet glorious." What I saw when I went to Lebanon in 1968 seemed sadly removed from the prophet's vision. Precariously clumped together on a small hillside, surrounded by bleak, arid mountains, the few remaining "trees of the Lord", still guarded by a Greek Maronnite father, covered too small an area to maintain the micro-climate essential for their survival. The diminutive area in a vast expanse of bare mountains once covered with cedars, ilex and cypresses needed (and still needs) to be supported and expanded with enlightened planting. The entire area required protection from goats and enlargement of the little nurseries in the nearby village to include helpful indigenous species of nurse trees.

I drove high over the mountains, just as the sun was rising, and looked down thousands of feet at the pathetic little patch of cedars, a mere spot of dark green in a parched and naked landscape. I wondered then if it could be in the mind of wealthy Jewry to compensate Lebanon by restoring her tree cover, the destruction of which was started by King Solomon some three thousand years ago.

I had been greatly looking forward to my return visit to the United Arab Republic but I was quite unprepared for the affectionate reunion awaiting me in Cairo where I was met by Hussein Zied, Director-General of Public Relations. Later I was received by General Hassan Sobeh, Director of the Desert Organization. A full day's visit to the Tahrir Province, the Liberation Province, was arranged. Here a whole network of canals had been laid out and large-scale land reclamation had been completed since my last visit in 1966. It was heartening to find that their reclamation programme had exceeded all expectations and that wide areas of desert, which two thousand years ago had been the granary of Rome, were now being made fruitful again.

I went on to Rome itself. Arriving there once more my mind went back to my first official visit there in 1926 when I was representing the Men of the Trees, and Nigeria, at the First World

Forestry Conference. I was met on that occasion by Rumann, former Resident of Benin.

I remembered how I had helped him to build a Roman Catholic Church for Benin. Rumann was a devout Catholic and had long considered that the time was ripe for a church to be built in Benin. He was about to retire and was anxious to see the thing done before he left. One evening he invited me to dinner and confided this ambition to me. "Will you help me to do this?" he pleaded. I agreed to provide the timber if he would arrange for an architect and for the actual building of the church. Eventually the church was completed and dedicated by the Bishop; and Rumann retired to Rome, happy to have achieved his long-felt wish. He sent me a figure for the cross from Rome, and with my own hands I fashioned a fine Iroko cross, mounted the figure upon it, and presented it to the Bishop for dedication.

Rumann was later decorated by the Pope with the Order of St. Gregory the Great for his outstanding missionary service to the Church. When he met me off my train in 1926 he took me straight to a private audience with Pope Pius XI, who was curious to see the English forester whose first book, *The Brotherhood of the Trees*, had been put on the *Index*, yet who had provided the timber for the first church to be built in Benin for four hundred years. I asked the Holy Father that morning if my book could be removed from the *Index*, explaining that the Men of the Trees was not a secret society as his Missionary Cardinal in India had thought. True, there was a particular handshake among the first *Watu wa Miti* and a password, but it was a fraternity like the Scouts, who also had a special salute and a special way of shaking hands, yet were not regarded as a secret society. The Holy Father turned to a Cardinal, saying a few words I did not understand. Nine months later the ban on my book was lifted.

From the Vatican I went to the reception for the First World Forestry Congress being given by Mussolini and the King—the former, dynamic and obviously interested in the foresters he was receiving from all over the world; the King, friendly enough but jaded and somewhat bored, little realizing, I imagine, that he was helping to make history, for this was the first time there had ever been a gathering of foresters from sixty-two countries. They had come together to pool information about the forest resources of the world and to see what could be done to stem the threatened timber famine.

That afternoon Rumann, 'the Count' as we called him, and an Australian lady whose son was studying architecture in Rome, organized a *thé dansant* in my honour at the Swiss Hotel. Douglas Fairbanks and Mary Pickford were also being entertained at the same hotel and our parties got mixed up. For the second time the same day I was presented to the Duce, who was alone and relaxed. He chatted about the Forestry Congress and asked me about my work in the mahogany forests of Nigeria, I told him of my meeting with his Consul in Nigeria, Dr. Conviccione, whom I had invited to lunch to see a march-past of the first Men of the Trees. Seeing them, Dr. Conviccione had exclaimed excitedly: "This is marvellous, Baker! You must meet my friend Mussolini!" I also told the Duce about my first visit to Italy in 1923, when I had been met by members of his *Partito Nationale* to whom I had suggested that Rome would be an ideal centre for the first World Forestry Congress, which even then I had been hoping to convene. I hoped he could see my delight that this had now happened.

While we were talking we had been studying each other closely— we felt sure that we had met before—years before—some time shortly after World War I. Yes, in Soho—it was he who remembered first. While learning English in London he had sometimes waited at a restaurant. Was it the *Rendezvous*? Yes, indeed. I had frequently been there when I was entertaining special friends. While we were discovering this we had been drinking tea; I handed him some sandwiches.

"The first time I met you," he said, "I had the pleasure of waiting upon you. Now you are returning the compliment!"

Now I was in Rome again, this time expressly for an audience with Pope Paul, and to see Dr. Sen, Director-General of the F.A.O. I was representing the Moncivitam, World Parliament at the Conference of Parliamentarians in Geneva and had come on to Florence and Vallombrosa where in 1926, I had taken my fellow members of the World Forestry Congress to admire the forest. It had been planted on the mountainside by the old monks who, when it was bleak and bare, had chiselled holes in the rocky sides,

filling them with good earth carried up from the valley in sacks;
into each hole they had tucked a little fir or beech. Here at
Vallambrosa Milton had conceived the idea of *Paradise Lost*. I
wished I could stay a while at his home in the mountains to enjoy
the solitude of this woodland sanctuary. But there were deserts
waiting to be reclaimed and I wanted to get the Holy Father's
blessing for this work.

In Rome my first visit was to the British Embassy to register for
a ticket for the Vatican.

"How long are you staying in Rome?" inquired the Private
Secretary.

"Three days," I answered.

"It takes at least three weeks to get an audience," said the
Secretary.

Sadly I took my departure and returned to my hotel. The next
morning I was on the point of telephoning a Canadian Cardinal
friend when I saw an American couple, dressed in black, waiting in
the lobby.

"Lucky you," I said, as I wished them good morning, "I know
where you are going."

"Yes," said the lady, "my husband gave a church in New York.
Our friend at the Vatican said we should go early to get the best
place in the front row. Would you care to join us?—we have two
extra tickets. But we have to leave in five minutes."

Would I care to join them!? Needless to say, I was ready in no
time at all.

At the end of the audience the Cardinal, Master of Ceremonies,
said that the Holy Father would be pleased to bless anything we
treasured. I had no rosary or crucifix, not even a prayer book—but
I had one precious copy of *Sahara Challenge*, which I had brought
to present to the Director-General of F.A.O.

As the Pope passed I knelt with my book raised in front of me
and he blessed it. After the audience I telephoned the Cardinal and
said: "Monsignor, I have a confession to make."

I told him what I had done and continued:

"Is it too much to hope that in a future encyclical the Holy
Father will mention that the most pressing need of the world today
is to reclaim the deserts and feed the people?"

"Now, Baker," said the Cardinal, "you must not ask me what the Pope will say in his next encyclical. However, I am sure that when I tell his Holiness of your fine work in the Sahara he will certainly pray for you and the success of your work in reclaiming the deserts to feed the people."

I thanked him and said how relieved I was. It was as though a great weight of responsibility had been lifted from me. I felt like a little man carrying a huge, heavy load up a steep hill who is picked up by a man in a comfortable car and driven to the top.

After that I hurried to the headquarters of F.A.O., for I had an appointment with Dr. Sen, and time was running short. Apologizing for being late, I said I had only just left the Vatican and felt sure that if Dr. Sen knew I was here he would give me a few minutes. I had travelled all the way from New Zealand for this appointment with him.

"Come in, Baker," said Dr. Sen, "I have been waiting for you. We met last in New Delhi when you were working out your shelter-belt scheme for my country with Nehru."

I entered and took the seat he indicated. "What is on your mind, Baker?" he asked quietly.

I said: "On Tuesday next, fifteen countries of the Sahara will be appealing to you for help in planning to contain the desert threatening them. The last chapter of this book, *Sahara Challenge*, has an over-all plan for Sahara Reclamation and I want you to have this before your Symposium on Tuesday. This is the only copy I have in Europe and it has just been blessed by the Holy Father. I feel you should have it."

I handed the book to him, and he said: "Thank you. Please inscribe it for me."

A year later I was addressing a representative audience in Brisbane including members from many progressive societies. My subject was "Sahara Reclamation and How it could Relieve World Tensions". In the evening newspaper there was a tiny paragraph dated the previous day. The Pope addressing the United Nations Assembly in New York had said: "It is not enough to dole out rations of food to the starving millions—we must give the emerging countries technical aid. We must help them to reclaim the deserts and feed the people." It was with a feeling of profound gratitude I

quoted these words, which had so recently been broadcast throughout the world; and when I went back to Rome in October 1968, I
renewed my contacts with F.A.O., making appointments with the
new Director-General and the newly appointed Head of the World
Food Organization who were to plan and work together to make
the world's most famous desert fruitful again.

Now, however, I went back to England where I was able to
spend time with my son Paul. He had won a place at Caius College,
Cambridge, my old college, and I wanted to show him round the
place. It was difficult to say which of the two of us was the more
excited!

Chapter 12

FOR THE HEALING OF NATIONS

I am here upon this Earth
To reclaim the Earth
To turn the desert into Paradise
A Paradise most suitable unto God
And His Associates to dwell thereon.

Ainyahita: *Wisdom from the Past.*
c. 10,000 B.C.

IN THE FIRST CHAPTER I described my first cosmic experience which I had as a child. My second cosmic experience was while I was in my dentist's chair. Peter Evans was an early member of the Men of the Trees—I had been introduced to him by Violet Culme-Seymour, a Founding Member who, with Ursula Grant-Duff, the first Hon. Secretary, was present at "Thriplands", Kensington Court, on November 4, 1924, the foundation day of the Men of the Trees in England. Peter Evans' dentist's chair very soon became popular with members. When I was in Nigeria, people going on leave would ask me to give them an introduction to a good dentist and I had no hesitation in recommending Peter and so his surgery became a place of reunion for my friends. His work was first-class and his fees reasonable.

During the war he used to devote a day a week to meeting his clients at Oxford, where he used the surgery of a friendly dentist. Once he attended to me there and as I was leaving I saw a notice:

WILL CLIENTS KINDLY SETTLE FOR WORK DONE BEFORE LEAVING AS IT SAVES BOOK-KEEPING IN WARTIME.

I pointed to this notice and said to Peter: "What's the damage? May I see your secretary?" to which he replied:

"St. Barbe, I would not dream of taking another fee from you. Last week your book *Trees Book of the Seasons* arrived at Onslow Gardens. I was tidying up the surgery when the postman arrived and one of the family shouted: 'St. Barbe's book has come,' and they took it down into the underground living room to open the parcel. I followed and we were all looking at your book when a bomb dropped just outside my surgery wiping that part of the house away while we were all safe below. Your book saved all our lives and that is why I should never dream of taking another fee from you".

This book has been called a "wartime escape book". It was the sort of book for a bedside table. Its poetry and tree lore was restful during raids and the stress and strain of war. On that afternoon it proved to be an escape book in a different sense.

Twice a year I would take my small daughter Angela to Peter for the usual inspection. By this time he had gone up in the world and his surgery was at the top of a fine building in Portman Square. He would pump the chair up as far as it would go and point out the B.B.C. in Portland Place, admire her teeth and let her down again. The last time but one I sat in this chair I saw farther than the B.B.C. for I had been given gas for an extraction. I breathed the magic ether and entered the land of dreams. My vision was of a huge nine-pointed star and from each of the points was a beam lighting up symbols of the nine religions of the world; as the great star revolved the emblems of the world faiths moved too and each in turn came into full vision. As I was coming round I begged Peter to take out another tooth so that I could see the end of this glorious vision that had been vouchsafed to me; but he protested:

"St. Barbe, you can't afford to have another tooth out just for the sake of enjoying a beatific vision!"

So I asked if I might be allowed to rest for a while so that I might try and draw what I had just seen. It was more than I could manage so I told an artist what I had seen and he said he could paint it and the fee would be twenty guineas. How I wish I had been able to commission it!

For the next two years the vision of the nine-pointed star was vividly in my mind; at dawn it inspired me in my meditation and as I closed my eyes to sleep it seemed to draw me upwards towards its light until I was absorbed into its very heart.

When the time came for me to have another extraction I prayed that I might be permitted to carry on from the nine-pointed star and see beyond.

I inhaled deep breaths of the magic elixir and, entering the world of the spirit saw a vision which I could not adequately describe if I lived for a thousand years. The central part was a broad highway lined with beautiful trees radiating all the colours of the rainbow. Each tree bore all the fruits known to me and many others I had never seen before. The nine-pointed star was situated at the end of the road and drew me towards it and in the distance there were parks and gardens with rare trees from many countries and friends of all colours and creeds. Dominating the gardens of delight was the Tree of Life with leaves for the healing of the Nations.

This time I did not ask for more gas for I had been transported into heavenly places with bliss beyond description. I had seen the Garden of Paradise and could not conceive of any greater bounty.

Early in 1970 I visited again my old forestry stations at Benin and Sapoba in the mahogany forests of Nigeria, where forty-five years ago I was allowed to introduce silvicultural systems to change a wasting asset into an ever-increasing source of real wealth. It was most moving to re-establish affectionate relations with some of my old forest rangers, workers and learners—more often than not with their sons and grandsons! Several had attained important government posts; Prince Edison A. Bagini-Eweka, my houseboy in 1925-6, had reached the exalted position of Paymaster. He came to Sapoba to see me in his fine car and brought members of his family with him.

Despite the difficult times Nigeria has been through recently and all the resultant disruption, I found everybody keen on all aspects of reconstruction. The University of Ibadan is carrying on the forestry research I initiated at Sapoba; it is now open to receive research students from the eighteen other countries of the Sahara. My dreams for the reclamation of the Sahara seem to be on their way to being realized.

This, as everyone knows, is European Conservation Year. Over twenty countries are taking part in a conference in Strasbourg; in London the Duke of Edinburgh is presiding at a national conference which is considering the main themes of conservation. It must be gratifying to Britishers to know that our planning and conservation laws are the envy of many other countries. Our outlook, however, is mainly aesthetic; we still have much to learn on the practical value of tree cover. Nevertheless we are fortunate in having such enthusiastically supported organisations as the National Trust and the Men of the Trees, which anyone can join and thus help to maintain a healthy, as well as beautiful environment in this wonderful country.

Chapter 13

THE PLANET IN DANGER

*"The angel cried with a loud voice, saying, Hurt not the earth,
neither the sea, nor the trees."*

Revelation 7:3

AT LONG LAST I am beginning to see a tree sense coming into being all over the world. Forty-five years ago in response to the China Inland Mission's request, I sent quantities of pine seed to raise trees for beauty, shelter and shade. Today those trees are yielding seed for some of the gigantic planting now taking place. Heartened as I had been by the Russian response in trebling the length of the shelter belt I had planned for President Roosevelt, it was an exhilarating experience to learn that the foresters of China have made a shelter belt six hundred and eighty miles long to stop the sands of the Gobi Desert spreading into China proper, and that the Old Wall of China was becoming a tree wall stretching for two thousand miles. Members of the Men of the Trees in Melbourne on a visit to China brought back pictures showing millions of little trees like a green mist stretching as far as the eye could see on either side of that great rugged wall. Latest reports would indicate that as many as thirty-two million people are employed permanently in afforestation and that during the planting season about half of the white-collar brigade in the cities don their oldest clothes and go out into the country to help the peasants plant trees on the mountain-sides.

Peking, which was once tree-less, has now become a city of trees with avenues comprised of up to ten rows of trees. Large trees are often moved into position during the night; citizens sometimes wake to find that their road which was tree-less the night before is now tree-lined! The latest reports show that tree cover has been increased from seven per cent to twenty-seven per cent. This should bring great reassurance and set an example which all the world might follow.

Tree-planting is closely associated with the love of one's country and it is interesting to see that in People's China the care and planting of trees has become the main pastime in the schools and recreation over the weekends for perhaps the greater part of the population. To inspire this there must have been widespread education as to the biological contribution trees make to life; there must be a sympathetic feeling for the earth and a desire to restore the Earth's Green Mantle. I have indications that there is a growing desire throughout the world to co-operate in a gigantic tree-planting programme not only in the Sahara but in a green belt to encircle the globe.

In one of his speeches as Prime Minister, Sir Winston Churchill might have foreseen the coming together of the peoples as a World Brotherhood of Tree Planting and a better understanding of God in Nature when he said:

"In the past we had a light which flickered; in the present we have a light which flames, and in the future there will be a light which shines over all the lands and sea."

We have been given guidance by President Roosevelt in his four essential freedoms on which the New World must be founded: the first is freedom of speech and expression—everywhere in the world. The second is freedom of every person to worship his Creator in his own way, everywhere in the world. The third is freedom from want, which, translated into world terms means economic understanding which will secure to every nation a healthy, peaceful life for the inhabitants. The fourth is freedom from care—meaning a world-wide reduction of armaments to such a point and in such a thorough fashion that no nation will be in a position to commit an act of physical aggression against a neighbour or another country, anywhere in the world. Spiritual values must be restored. Everything is spiritual which tends to understanding; towards kindness; towards thought which is productive of beauty; and of those things which lead man on to a fuller expression of his divine potentialities.

Of the earth's thirty billion acres already more than nine billion acres are desert. Land is being lost to agriculture and forestry much faster than it is being reclaimed. At the same time the world population is exploding. Already half the human family is on the verge of starvation, for man breeds and lives beyond the limits of the land. Yet if the armies of the world, now numbering twenty-two million, could be re-deployed in planting in the desert, in eight years a hundred million people could be rehabilitated and supplied with protein rich food grown from virgin sand.

The present is full of opportunity. Never before in the history of the planet has mankind been given the privileges and opportunities that are at his disposal today. A great light has been raised and is penetrating the darkness of the world, but alas, too many with dust blinded eyes have yet to catch the vision. Some of us have. That is our privilege and our responsibility.

The fate of an individual or a nation will always be determined by the degree of his or its harmony with the forces and laws of Nature and the universe. Man is not alone in the universe but is surrounded by sources of power, harmony and knowledge. The fullness of life depends upon man's harmony with the totality of the natural cosmic laws. Our individual evolution is a job that has to be carried on day by day by each individual himself. It is a lifelong task.

The conception of the Men of the Trees and Tree Lovers, as well as Lovers of Animals and Nature, is that of one great family going forward into the future, believing in a harmless way of life and enjoying beauty without cruelty, one humanity chastened, disciplined and illumined.

Too often the isolationist and racial attitudes are characteristic of the separist tendencies against which we of the Men of the Trees, with other progressive movements, are making a stand. We must be sympathetic to all. To understand we must first learn from each other and strengthen our bonds of friendship in service for our fellow men. We need new loyalties. Man as an individual or a nation does not reach maturity until a cause is discovered in which he or a nation can unite in a great endeavour which will defy years and outlast time itself. There is a new comradeship of the Green Front against the deserts of the world—the deserts of our own making. It may be that Africa will lead the way. It was Augustine, Bishop of Hippo in the fourth century who said:

"There is always some new thing coming out of Africa."

A forest is a perfect example of the law of return in action. Trees give back to the earth more than they take, while building up humus, and enriching the soil by the minerals thathave been carried up to the leaves in the rising sap. By nature man is a forest dweller. He was cradled in the tropics. His food was the fruit of trees. He possessed the secret of adaption to his environment, so that health, gentleness, beauty and strength were enjoyed to the full. In his forest setting man was conscious of his relationship to God and of his unity with all living things.

The memory of that Golden Age has come down through the ancient Egyptians, the earlier Greeks, the Aztecs, and is told in the folk-lore of African peoples of today.

The paradise or garden was a clearing in the forest where gourds and other vegetables were grown. The folk-lore and legends of the Golden Age echo the scriptures of many religions and show that trouble first came when man forsook the garden culture and became a herdsman. The traditional "field" or "felled" was a clearing in the forest. In the garden man lived in harmony with Nature and learned to understand the seasons for sowing and harvest; he would select his seed and, after sowing, protect it from birds, rodents, insects and sun. He would discover the best ways of storing his seed and food, and from the art of horticulture other forms of culture grew, with seasonal dances. As his techniques developed he gradually improved the flowering plants and developed edible grains such as wheat, barley and rye; stores and granaries were erected; fields were enlarged; more and more forest was removed and frequently the water cycle was broken. It took time for him to recognize the connection between tree cover and the growth of food crops. In the course of centuries man discovered it was easier to raise and graze domesticated animals than to hunt the wild ones. Soon flocks and herds spread over the land. The animals, especially goats, denuded ever-widening areas of trees. In order to protect their flocks the owners hunted for wolves and other predators. When the grass grew sparse they felled more forest, cutting and burning to make new grazing lands. The pressure on the land encouraged hamlets to swell into towns, and towns into cities, where the inhabitants developed trades and professions, demand for meat increased and crops were diverted to feed animals and walls were built around settlements to keep the animals out.

The Ancients believed that the earth was a sentient being and

responded to the behaviour of man upon it. As we have no scientific
proof to the contrary, should we not accept this point of view and
behave accordingly?

I look at it like this: if a man loses one-third of his skin he dies;
the plastic surgeons say, "He's had it." If a tree loses one-third of
its bark it dies. This has been proved scientifically by botanists and
dendrologists. Would it not be reasonable to suggest that if the
earth loses more than a third of its green mantle and tree cover, it
will assuredly die? The water table will sink beyond recall and life
will become impossible.

Already the most 'civilized' countries have almost reached that
fatal third. In the Author's Note to *The Coming Water Famine*,
Congressman Jim Wright says:

"In the United States today it takes three hundred gallons of
the indispensable fluid to produce a single loaf of bread. To grow a
pound of beef and to get it to your dinner table requires at least
one thousand gallons of water. About one hundred thousand
gallons go into the manufacture of each automobile .... The
harsh truth is that in the midst of unprecedented plenty America
is running out of usable water—not slowly, but rapidly. No
imaginable crisis could present a bleaker prospect."

I have been in New York after a four month drought when
there was a warning that in another month the entire metropolis
could be completely out of water "if it does not rain". "A fifty-
dollar fine is imposed upon the offering of a glass of water in a
restaurant, and residents are urged to take showers rather than
baths and to take them as seldom as possible," says the Congressman. He claims, too, that twenty billion gallons of water a day are
being wasted in the U.S.A. by pollution. This is water that could
be used and re-used if treated properly. "It offends the nose and
eyes of all who come near it, and it flows useless past water-hungry
communities on its way to an indifferent sea."

I have observed eight forms of pollution. There are ordinary
sewage and related organic substances, disease carrying infectious
agents, chemical plant nutrients, synthetic-organic chemicals,
sediment, radio-active substances, inorganic chemicals and mineral
substances, and heat. Any form singly may not be serious but
when these forms of pollution combine and act together in concert,

they often create a chemical mess which science cannot unravel and which, therefore, defies all purifying plants. Chemical fertilizers and pesticides find their way into the water. It has been pointed out that more than forty-five thousand pesticide formulæ are now registered with the U.S.A. Department of Agriculture.

About eight million pounds of these deadly synthetics are purchased each year and distributed over thirty million acres of cropland. A great proportion of this finds its way into the rivers, as also a great proportion of the 25,317,000 tons of fertilizers which they put each year on their fields and gardens. But what about the Great Lakes in their neighbourhood where one out of every eight Americans and, across the border, one out of every three Canadians reside? Many millions more in both nations are directly affected by what happens in those lakes and their waters. Some of them are already dead or dying and the water level in all five lakes has dropped to the lowest point in recorded history.

From water and earth we came, and the future of mankind on this planet will be determined by respectful or disrespectful treatment of these basic elements.

Water must be a basic consideration in everything: forestry, agriculture and industry. The forest is the mother of the rivers. First we must restore the tree cover to fix the soil, prevent too quick run-off, and steady springs, streams and rivers. We must restore the natural motion of our rivers and, in so doing, we shall restore their vitalizing functions. A river flowing naturally, with its bends, broads and narrows, has the motion of the blood in our arteries, with its inward rotation, tension and relaxation. Picture a river which has risen from a mountain spring in a well-treed watershed: trees of mixed species and different shaped roots; the spear-shaped roots, heart-shaped roots and flat roots—fixing the soil at different levels and reducing competition for food and water. The leaf-fall and humus on the floor of the forest will act as a sponge to retard quick run-off after a storm. Water will sink through to porous soil and form myriads of springs which will feed the land and the rivers during the drier months of the year. Mountains and high-ground should be covered with protective forests up to the snow-line; in high country, fields should be kept small and carved out of the forest and always be tree-surrounded.

How strange it is that communities fail to realize the importance of preserving tree cover on tree slopes. Man has a bad record as a forest destroyer, cutting and burning greedily and recklessly, destroying the built-up fertility that has accumulated through the centuries. He has been skinning the earth alive in his greed and folly and to satisfy his unnatural appetite for the flesh of his fellow creatures.

In some countries, such as the U.S.A., up to three-quarters of the land has been degraded to the use of growing crops to feed animals which they kill to feed themselves. Surely a round-about way of getting food, when it is possible to get food for ourselves direct from the earth through fresh vegetables, fruit and nut-bearing trees.

Recent discoveries in the field of nutrition have shown that it is possible to produce meat and milk direct from the plant kingdom. These foods are not only of better taste, but richer and more wholesome—easy to prepare and cheaper to use. Above all, everybody who has his own piece of land can easily raise his own raw materials for these foods on his own land.

I picture village communities of the future living in valleys protected by sheltering trees on the high ground. They will have fruit and nut orchards and live free from disease and enjoy leisure, liberty and justice for all, living with a sense of their one-ness with the earth and with all living things.

Under existing systems food looms large and there is a constant threat of famine over wide areas, but if we treat reafforestation as seriously as we do national defence, and turn from an animal economy to a sylvan one, we shall be able to look forward confidently to the time when food will worry us as little as the air we breathe. Indeed, when we have every man under his own vine and fig tree in a perfect earth, beautified by complete landscape husbandry, then with St. Francis of Assisi we shall be able to say:

"Praise be, my Lord, for our Sister, Mother Earth, which does sustain and keep us and bringeth forth divers fruits and flowers of many colours and grass."